THE GREAT DEPRESSION

Hard Times in the Coal Region

HARRY M. BOBONICH

Copyright © 2009 by Harry M. Bobonich

All rights reserved. No part of this book shall be reproduced or transmitted in any form or by any means, electronic, mechanical, magnetic, photographic including photocopying, recording or by any information storage and retrieval system, without prior written permission of the publisher. No patent liability is assumed with respect to the use of the information contained herein. Although every precaution has been taken in the preparation of this book, the publisher and author assume no responsibility for errors or omissions. Neither is any liability assumed for damages resulting from the use of the information contained herein.

ISBN 0-7414-5774-1

Published by:
INFINITY
PUBLISHING.COM
1094 New DeHaven Street, Suite 100
West Conshohocken, PA 19428-2713
Info@buybooksontheweb.com
www.buybooksontheweb.com
Toll-free (877) BUY BOOK
Local Phone (610) 941-9999
Fax (610) 941-9959

Printed in the United States of America
Published December 2009

Also by Harry M. Bobonich

Seeing Around Corners:
How Creative People Think

Big Mine Run:
Recollections of the Coal Region

World War II: Memories of a GI

Pathfinders and Pioneers:
Women in Science, Math and Medicine

For Gloria

Contents

Introduction — xiii

Late 1929

October 1929 – Wall Street Crashes — 1
Hard Times — 4

The Early 1930s

Hobos – Riding the Rails — 20
The Bonus Army — 31
Hoover's Last Months in Office — 36
Franklin Delano Roosevelt Becomes President — 44
Our Boarder Mike — 56
On Relief — 58
Bargains Everywhere — 65
Making Do — 69
Dynamite (duley) Boxes — 77
Pack Rats — 77
Layaway Plan — 78
Bartering — 78
FDR's First 100 Days — 80

The Civilian Conservation Corps (CCC)	81
Wally Baran	83
Lynchings	85

The Early Mid-1930s

The Bast Colliery and "Bootlegging Coal"	90
Anthracite Coal Breakers	106
Christmas Time	107
Easter	111
Mom	112
Making Soap	114
Quitting School	114
The Economy Still Depressed	117
Works Progress Administration (WPA)	127
Social Security	134
Women Step Up	135
Migrant Mother	148
The Model T	151
Minersville and the Supreme Court	153
Having Babies	160
Mealtime	163
Stealing Milk	166
Hunting and Fishing	170

Soup and More Soup	171
Making "Bums' Soup"	172
Jarring (Canning)	173

The Late Mid-1930s

FDR's First Term	175
After School	180
When the Junkman Came Around	180
When the Peddlers Came Around	181
Making Braided Rugs	182
Store at Your Door	183
The Beginning of FDR's Second Term	184
The Victrola	188
Listening to the Radio	189
Picking Huckleberries (Blueberries)	191
Picking Mushrooms	192
Summer Vacation	193
A Depression Within a Depression	198

The Late 1930s

My Summer in a Coal Hole	201
Joe Baldino and the Donkey	202
Homemade Candy	204

Homemade Soda	205
Making Wine	205
Making Moonshine	206
FDR and Civil Rights	212
Playing Games	219
Guerney (Gike) Buhl	222
Miners Despair	226
Making Our Own Play Things	231
Going to the Movies	233
The Depression Continues	234
Sledding Downhill	242
The Circus Is in Town	244
Going to the Carnival	245
Playing Cards	246
The Old Swimming Hole	246

The Early 1940s

Bootlegging Coal Still Going Strong	248
Hilbert Kroh's Story	251
War In Europe	253
Government Spending Continues	254
Our Family Situation Improving	255
FDR's Third Term	255

America Goes to War	259
Then and Now	260
FDR's Legacy	260
President Obama's Administration	261

Appendix

Some Highlights of the WPA	262
Acknowledgments	271
References	274
Music	275
Photo Credits	275
Notes	277
Peerless Furniture Company Letter	277

INTRODUCTION

"Hallelujah, I'm a Bum"

Oh, why don't you work
Like other men do?
How the hell can I work
When there's no work to do?

–Anonymous

It is far better to recall the Great Depression than it was to live through it. This book, then, is a recollection of those hard times that I remember growing up during those turbulent years. As it turned out, the Depression lasted for about 11 years, from late 1929 to 1941.

In this book I describe how my family got by during that decade – the most devastating economic catastrophe in American history. I do not focus on the big story about the Great Depression; I deal with the day-in and day-out problems of living (or better, "making-do") during those uncertain times. The desolation of the Depression, however, knew no boundaries. Many, many people suffered; some more than others.

This is a snapshot of life growing up in a coal-mining "patch" called Big Mine Run located in Schuylkill County, Pennsylvania during the 1930s. I do include some national economic and political issues that I feel are relevant to these experiences, and I have included stories from friends and acquaintances of what their grandmothers and grandfathers told them about how it was "back then."

I also have numerous human-interest stories from newspapers of those years. They depict the hard times of thousands of ordinary and not-so-ordinary people who lived through the Great Depression. It was a time that called for unprecedented courage in an unprecedented crisis. These stories tell of the daily struggles of people who coped (and those who could not deal) with one of the worst decades in American history.

Finally, I have included a broad spectrum of photographs, which show a side of the Depression that only pictures can convey.

Through it all, those remarkable, resilient survivors of the Great Depression worked their way through it. They did what had to be done.

Perhaps those today who feel they, too, are living in similarly difficult economic times can take heart in knowing that they will get through the "bad times." After all, you grandchildren of today have some of your grandparents' "survival genes," and that's saying a lot. The trick: Whatever has to be done, just do it.

Late 1929

October 1929 – Wall Street Crashes

Arguably, the stock market collapse started on Wednesday, Oct. 23, 1929, when stock prices fell sharply. The Dow Jones Industrial Average (DJIA), informally the Dow, dropped about 21 points, or 6 percent. On the following day there was panic selling on Wall Street. A record 13 million shares were traded. By the end of the day, however, the Dow had only dropped six points, about 2 percent.

Nevertheless the tone was set, the stock market was nervous and the massive selling was a sign that things would get worse. Historically, Thursday, Oct. 24, is known as Black Thursday. On Friday and the half day session on Saturday, the Dow held firm (the stock market was open on Saturday during those days).

Then on Monday, Oct. 28, the Dow dropped 13 percent. On the following day, the Dow continued its downward spiral, falling another 31 points (12 percent).

The Dow closed on Tuesday, Oct. 22 at 326.5; on the following Tuesday, Oct. 29, it closed at 230.1, a decline of 30 percent. Tuesday, Oct. 29, when 16 million shares were traded, is also referred to as Black Tuesday. Within three weeks the value of stocks on the New York Stock Exchange fell by 40 percent.

That short period of time precipitated a financial panic, which marked the beginning of years of "hard times." In three months, unemployment almost doubled. It was 5 percent in October and increased to 9 percent by December 1929, and it continued to increase. The effect of the stock market crash quickly spread worldwide. President Herbert Hoover had only been in office for eight months (in July of 1927 when Calvin Coolidge was president, unemployment was only 3.3 percent). The Great Depression left an indelible mark on Hoover's presidency.

While I don't remember anything specific about those several days, it is the beginning of my story of the long, difficult Great Depression.

Headlines from national newspapers as they covered the crash:

The Washington Post, Oct. 29, 1929:

BANKERS PLAN TO AID AS STOCKS COLLAPSE TO NEW LEVELS

The New York Times, Oct. 30, 1929:

STOCKS COLLAPSE IN 16,410,030-SHARE DAY, BUT RALLY AT CLOSE CHEERS BROKERS BANKERS OPTIMISTIC, TO CONTINUE AID

The Philadelphia Inquirer, Oct. 30, 1929:

STOCK CRASH HALTED AFTER PRICES SAG IN 16,410,030-SHARE DAY

Los Angeles Times, Oct. 30, 1929:

STOCKS DIVE AMID FRENZY IN 16,410,000-SHARE DAY

The *Shenandoah Evening Herald,* Oct. 30, 1929:

Wall Street Will Receive No Aid From Washington

Robert C. Albright
United Press Correspondent

Washington, Oct. 30. (U.P.) – Wall Street must work out its own salvation without hope of material aid from the government, according to the interpretation placed today on the failure of the Federal Reserve System to move to check the tide of stock sales, or make any formal statement or policy alteration.

Many who formerly urged that the central bankers maintain a "hands-off" policy when prices were at their peak and the re-discount issue paramount, now are looking to Washington for action in the present emergency. It is rapidly becoming apparent to observers here, however, that there is little the board could do to alleviate the situation.

Hard Times

Following the stock market crash of October 29, 1929, investors lost large amounts of money and some simply lost everything (less than 2 percent of adults owned stocks at the time, while approximately 50 percent owned stocks in the fall of 2008). My parents did not have any investments and it is likely that no one else in Big Mine Run did either. When you don't have any money, you don't have to worry about losing it.

Still, the following period of very low business activity and high unemployment was long and very difficult. Many stores, factories and banks closed; that left millions of people in poverty. Countless numbers of people had to depend on the government for food.

1. Notice to unemployed workers.

The *Shenandoah Evening Herald,* Nov. 13, 1929:

Two Children From Mill Creek Found Begging in Town

Mary Matskus, aged 11, and Joseph Matskus, aged 13, both claiming residence at Mill Creek, were picked up on the streets here this morning and turned over to the police.

The children, who claim to be the son and daughter of Mr. and Mrs. William Kupstus, their mother being married for the second time, were soliciting money from persons on the streets.

When questioned about their appearance in town, the children explained that they had started to walk to Frackville and after traveling a short distance on foot secured a ride on a bus to Shenandoah.

The boy had about $1.50 in his pocket, which he said was secured by begging on the streets. The girl was rather shy while the boy told several conflicting stories about their adventure in town. Both claimed that about two months ago the family moved from Ringtown and settled at Mill Creek.

Joseph stated that his mother had told him to leave home with his sister at an early hour this morning for the purpose of begging for money. He also said that his mother gave him some money and the remainder had been secured from pedestrians.

The local police will return the children to their home. There are six other children in the family, the boy stated.

The *Shenandoah Evening Herald*, Dec. 2, 1929:

Parents Jailed for Cruelty to Children

Claiming that Mr. and Mrs. Adolph Kowalczyk had forced their five minor children out of the house into freezing weather last Friday night, the couple was placed under arrest by Lieut. Joe Hentz on Saturday morning on a charge of cruelty and neglect of their children.

The couple was taken before Justice Joseph Miernicki, who ordered the pair removed to the county jail in default of $300 bail.

According to the story told to police who investigated the affair, Kowalczyk and his wife forced their five small children, ranging in age from eighteen months to 11 years, out into the cold weather last Friday night and subjected the children to the most extreme exposure while in a fit of intoxication.

Many complaints had been received by Lieut. Hentz from the neighborhood, it is said, and the affair on Friday night climaxed the situation as far as the father and mother are concerned.

The children were taken to the county home for children, where they will be cared for pending the outcome of the case in court.

2. A typical unemployment line (ca. 1929).

It wasn't only poor people who were out of work; the wave of unemployment rapidly enveloped the middle class as well, and it continued to rise in the ensuing months and years.

It was a time when men and women had to adapt to the difficult circumstances they were facing. In most cases, a change of employment was downward. People who were highly trained or well-educated were forced to take much lower-paying jobs. Any work was better than none, but in many cases, there was "no help needed."

3. No job, no hope.

According to Dr. John Fague, columnist for *The Shippensburg News-Chronicle*, the Peerless Furniture Company started making furniture in the spring of 1910. For 50 years it was an important part of the economy in Shippensburg, a small town in south central Pennsylvania.

Fague found the following letter while looking through William Burkhart's notebooks at the Shippensburg Historical Society. Carl A. Naugle was president of the Peerless plant when he wrote the "attention-getting" letter dated Nov. 5, 1930. The letter, while self-explanatory, is an example of working conditions during the Depression years.

PEERLESS FURNITURE COMPANY
INCORPORATED
MANUFACTURERS OF
DINING AND LIVING ROOM FURNITURE
SHIPPENSBURG, PA.

NEW YORK FURNITURE EXCHANGE
206 LEXINGTON AVENUE
NEW YORK CITY

AMERICAN FURNITURE MART
666 LAKE SHORE DRIVE
CHICAGO, ILL.

November 5, 1930

Mr. Employee, Peerless Furniture Company

Dear Sir:

"Times are hard", economists disagree as to relative statistics; but none may blink the fact that jobs are scarce, and that a man out of employment is out of luck.

Such conditions should force each of us—we who have jobs—to take stock of himself. If you are careless, there are dozens of careful men hammering at the doors for your job. If you are disloyal and disgruntled you should get out voluntarily and let a man have the job who would hail it as a godsend.

There need be no secret of the fact that Peerless is "tightening up". Slipshod, careless, indifferent work will no longer be tolerated. Disobedience of orders or regulations will result in instant dismissal. Peerless has reached this stage of the depression with flying colors; she will reach the end of it in exactly the same manner; but only the square shooting employee can be carried with her, and that's that.

You may take this as a plea or a threat, just as you choose. Employees of this Company have not been affected by the depression. You have been having a "boom" period rather than a "panic"—an unusual condition. For your information we insist that a job is a job, now-a-days, and should be valued as such.

Cost of living is coming down—wages, too. New York City paying 10,000 laborers $15.00 per week on city work. Why are you getting more than that?

We have not thought of a general wage cut at this time, we hope the time never comes when some of you have to be cut, but it will come some time. We have, however, a list of about ten men who will be told within the next week to look for other jobs or take a wage reduction, and we tell you now that we prefer your getting another job. The list may grow. Each man determines for himself.

We doubt our ability to keep up night work much longer. Hope we are wrong, but don't think so. A lesson from nature—squirrels put away nuts and bees store honey. Why? Rainy days do come.

This written after careful thought—and for your benefit rather than ours. It's an easy situation for us to handle, we assure you.

Take it, please, as a friendly personal letter.

Sincerely,

Peerless Furniture Company,

Carl A. Naugle

4. See appendix for typed copy.

Fague said Wayne Russell was employed by the Peerless Furniture Company in 1930. Wayne, who was 10 years old, earned 12.5 cents an hour.

Carl A. Naugle's sister-in-law, Louise Hoch Naugle, told Fague that her father, James Hoch, worked at the Peerless plant from 1931-33. He worked two days a week and received $5 for his weekly wage. Louise also told Fague that her brother, Roy, was only 14-years-old when he started to work at the Peerless plant in 1927. Roy was paid 16 cents an hour. She added that the hourly wage increased to 65 cents during World War II.

The Early 1930s

The *Shenandoah Evening Herald,* Oct. 29, 1930:

TREMONT GOES TO WASHINGTON ASKING AID

COLLIERIES IN WEST END HAVE CLOSED

By Lyle C. Wilson
United Press Staff Correspondent

Washington, Oct. 29. (U.P.) – The West End Civic Center of Tremont, Pa., has appealed for help in finding employment for 1,800 men to protect their wives and children from suffering. The men lost their jobs . . . when mines in the vicinity closed. The Civic Center suggested highway construction be initiated to provide employment.

The *Shenandoah Evening Herald,* Nov. 3, 1930:

FIFTH SUICIDE FROM BUSINESS REVERSES

Philadelphia, Nov. 3. (U.P.) – Business losses caused the fifth suicide here within 11 days, it was reported today.

The latest victim was Arthur H. Blackburn, 69, president and treasurer of the Oxford Bindery, Inc., whose body was found on a bench in Cloverly Park, Wissahickon yesterday.

Blackburn sent two bullets through his brain, causing almost immediate death. Decline in business and reverses on the stock market caused Blackburn considerable worry in recent months, members of the family reported.

5. Selling apples was a common sight.

Throughout the 1930s, the southwestern Great Plains region of the United States suffered a severe drought, and 19 states in the heartland of America became known as "the dust bowl." About 400,000 people left the Great Plains and traveled westward to find work and a better way of life for their families. These unfortunate families suffered terribly and were much worse off than we were in Big Mine Run and the Coal Region in general.

While the Great Depression affected virtually everyone, no group had it harder than African-Americans. Early in the 1930s, about half of all black Americans were unemployed. There were no African-Americans living in Big Mine Run and I don't recall that any lived in Ashland, a small town of about 7,000, which was only a mile to the west.

President Hoover did not respond to the economic crisis the country was facing soon enough. In his book, *Nothing to Fear*, historian Adam Cohen said, "[Hoover's] free-market ideology taught him that private enterprise should be the source of all solutions, and his near-religious commitment to 'rugged individualism' convinced him that giving aid to the Depression's victims would morally damage them."

The Smoot-Hawley Tariff bill, signed by Hoover in 1930, was the most protectionist legislation in the history of the United States. It fostered and developed domestic industries by protecting them from foreign competition through duties and quotas imposed on imported products. The tariff actually hurt, rather than helped, the economy. It virtually closed down America's borders to foreign goods and started a mutually damaging international trade war.

6. Men eating in a soup kitchen (ca. 1932).

The *Shenandoah Evening Herald,* Nov. 3, 1931:

WORRIED MOTHER KILLED CHILDREN

Philadelphia, Nov. 3. (U.P.) – While her husband was away from home looking for work today a 21-year-old mother worried over the lack of money and food in their home shot and killed her three children and then committed suicide.

The victims were Mrs. Anna Nathan; Charles, 5; Herbert, 4; and Eva, 2. Neighbors heard the shots in the Nathan home and notified police, who discovered the bodies. All were pronounced dead at the Temple University Hospital.

Police reported Mrs. Nathan had stuffed rags and papers in cracks of the doors and windows in her kitchen and turned on the jets in the gas range.

Apparently becoming impatient as the gas seeped from the stove she fired the fatal shots. The children were shot through the chests and she had two bullet wounds through her head.

The family was destitute, police said, the husband having been out of work for the last eight months. He had been employed previously as a chef at a lunch wagon.

Police said Mrs. Nathan's note to her husband explained that she no longer could withstand their impoverished condition and the starvation, which confronted her children.

7. Serving soup in high heels.

The *Shenandoah Evening Herald,* March 21, 1932:

TWELVE HUNDRED NEEDY SUPPLIED

Approximately 250 families, or an estimate of about 1,250 people, were given provisions at the relief store in the warehouse of the Columbia Brewing Company, South Ferguson street, today, when the actual work of dispensing foodstuffs to the poor and needy in the community commenced under the direction of the Shenandoah Welcome Association.

Early this morning, long lines of people who have been impoverished by continued unemployment, formed at the relief store and a force of workers comprised of members of the American Legion and the various fire companies were on hand to help Manager William Griffiths in distributing the foodstuffs.

The list of provisions that were distributed included potatoes, beans, coffee, syrup, sugar, oatmeal, milk, bread and meat.

Several persons generously donated the service of their automobiles to take the relief supplies to needy families in Wm. Penn, Lost Creek, Shenandoah Heights and other adjoining communities.

Only after dragging his feet for years did Hoover attempt to employ government intervention to improve the poor economic situation the country was facing. In the summer of 1932, Hoover got the federal government into the relief business with the Emergency Relief and Construction Act (ERA). Hoover's intervention programs passed by Congress and signed by Hoover did not help to improve the economy in a significant way.

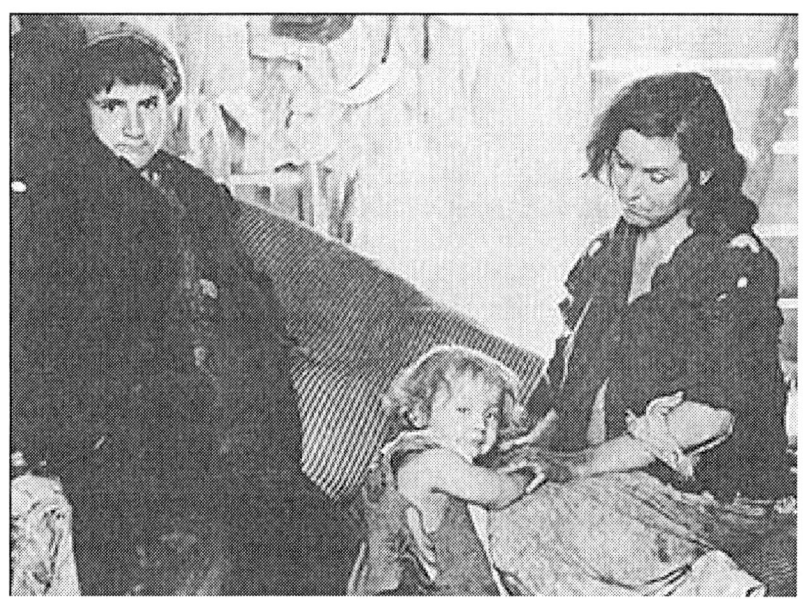

8. Homeless mother with her children.

The *Shenandoah Evening Herald*, July 19, 1932:

President Hoover's Pen
Today Set in Motion a $2
Billion Relief Plan

Several States are Already Moving to Obtain Their Share – Pennsylvania Asks for $10 million at Once and $35 million More Later

Washington, D.C., July 19. (U.P.) – One stroke of the pen by President Herbert Hoover today will set in motion a $2 billion relief program planned to provide food, shoes, and jobs for the unemployed man, with several states already moving to obtain their share of relief funds.

The president was ready to sign the measure, in which Congress committed the Federal Government to the most far-reaching relief plan in its history.

States that have reached the bottom of the relief resources will be lent a total of $300 million for direct relief of distress – for providing groceries, clothing, fuel and shelter for the destitute unemployed and their families.

Not only will this directly aid the unemployed, but also the Hoover Administration confidently believes it will be a boon to business generally, by creating demand for trainloads of materials and increase the purchasing power of the people.

In 1931 the Dow decreased by 52.7 percent, the largest single-year loss since its inception in 1896. The second largest decrease occurred in 1907 when the Dow fell by 37.7 percent. The third largest decrease occurred in 2008 with a decrease in the Dow of 33.8 percent. (The Dow reached a pre-crash high of 381.2 on Sept. 3, 1929. The first time it closed higher at 382.7 was on Nov. 23, 1954, some 25 years later).

9. Getting along somehow (ca.1929).

The "Great Depression" was originally called the "Great Panic." President Hoover, however, felt the word "panic" was too severe, so he substituted the word "depression."

Hoover did not have the political skill to deal with the depression. Also, he lacked the ability to deliver reassuring speeches. He did try, however, to make the nation feel more optimistic by asking Rudy Vallee, a popular singer, to come up with a Hoover campaign song. Vallee chose a song called, "Brother, Can You Spare a Dime?" The song was from the musical "Americana," which opened on Broadway in 1932. Unfortunately, the song did not distract the people from thinking about the hard times they were facing. Instead, it reminded them even more about the despair and uncertainty in their lives. In addition to Vallee, Bing Crosby also recorded a popular version of the song (and if you visit YouTube online, you can hear as well as feel the sadness of the Depression in the lyrics).

> They used to tell me I was building a dream
> And so I followed the mob.
> When there was earth to plow or guns to bear,
> I was always there, right on the job.
> They used to tell me I was building a dream
> With peace and glory ahead –
> Why should I be standing in line, just waiting for bread?
>
> Once in khaki suits,
> Gee, we looked swell,
> Full of that Yankee Doodle de-dum.
> Half a million boots went sloggin' through Hell,
> I was the kid with the drum.
> Say, don't you remember, they called me Al –
> It was Al all the time.
> Say, don't you remember, I'm your pal –
> Brother, can you spare a dime?

Hobos – Riding the Rails

The *Shenandoah Evening Herald,* Dec. 20, 1929:

Shenandoah
Entertained
Hobo King

"All hail the King!" Royalty has visited Shenandoah in the form of J. Leon Lazarowitz, king of hoboes, monarch of all he surveys as well as being the leader of some 1,889 other "Knights of the Road," who was re-elected to the "elevated" position at the annual meeting of hobos which was held at Chicago on Nov. 5.

"King" Lazarowitz carries his crown in his pocket, but it is not made of jewels and gold as most crowns are made of, but of plain white cardboard fitting, to the position he holds.

The leader of the tribe of roamers also stated that he admired the American women for their beauty and that the girls of this section are very attractive as compared to some sections.

He was impressed with the people of Shenandoah and stated that they were very sociable and treated him with the best while in town. Besides the United States, he would sooner roam about Canada or Australia.

The origin of the word "hobo" is unclear, although there are several possibilities. One suggestion, by author Todd DePastion, is that it came from "hoe-boy," which means farmhand, or a greeting like, "Ho, boy!" Another suggestion, from *Made in America*, by Bill Bryson, is that it came form the railroad greeting, "Ho beau" or from the syllabic abbreviation of "homeward bound."

10. Hobos riding the rails.

During the Great Depression, about one million young men (hobos) were traveling across the country hopping on and off of freight trains illegally, seeking work that didn't exist. They ranged in age from about 16 to 25. Surprisingly, there also were a small number of women who rode the rails, mostly dressed in men's clothes.

Many hobos left home seeking employment, but a few left for other reasons. Some felt they were a burden to their family and left, others were seeking a better way of life, and some were simply bored and pursuing adventure. As unemployment increased, more hobos rode the rails.

Many men who had been successful in their careers were now destitute and recipients of charity. Past wealth and prestige did not count. Now they were getting free transportation provided by the railroad company. A *Life* magazine cartoon depicted two hobos riding on a boxcar.

One said to the other, "It seems like only yesterday that I had stock in this company."

Since hopping on and off of a fast-moving freight train was dangerous, a large number of hobos were injured or killed. Some estimate that as many as 5,000 were killed each year. In addition, the railroad owners hired brutal guards, called "bulls," to keep the hobos off of the trains. They wanted paying customers only.

The hobos had a network of camps near the railroads. They would hop from the freight they were riding and after spending a short time in camp they would be on their way again. The camps almost always had a source of running water – they could make coffee, soup or just get a drink.

11. Hobo making turtle soup.

Hobos had their own vocabulary, code and set of ethical standards. "Bo," was the common expression one hobo used to refer to another. The "Jungle" was an area adjacent to a railroad where hobos camped or hung out. They also developed a set of markings to keep each other informed. A wavy line (marked by chalk or some other tool) meant water; when the wavy line was drawn above an X, it signified water and a campsite. One of their ethical standards was to help runaway children by trying to get them to return home.

Some that rode the rails became famous later in life: Eric Sevareid, the journalist; Supreme Court Justice William O. Douglas; TV host Art Linkletter; oil billionaire H.L. Hunt, and writers Jack London and Carl Sandburg.

In the early 1930s, when I was about 9 or 10 years old, I visited a hobo's camp along with several other kids. It was located one-quarter of a mile from our home, adjacent to the Reading Railroad Line that ran east and west past Big Mine Run. The hobos would be sitting on the ground next to a small fire heating coffee or making some kind of watery soup. They would often talk to us and I never found any of them unfriendly.

During one of my visits, a very young hobo (probably too young to be a hobo) took out his harmonica and start playing a tune. I didn't know the song, but it sounded sad and it may have been the "Hobo Blues." If you visit YouTube online you can hear it.

> When I first thought to Hobo'in, Hobo'in,
> I took a freight train to be my friend, O Lord.
> You know I hoboed, hoboed, hoboed,
> Hoboed, a long, long way from home, O Lord.

12. Teenagers riding the rails.

    I was too young to be a hobo. When I was about 12 years old I heard the older kids bragging about hopping aboard freight trains as they traveled past Big Mine Run. It sounded like an adventurous thing to try; I didn't realize that it was a dangerous thing to do. It is difficult to hop aboard a moving freight train, even if it is not moving very fast. When attempting to hop aboard, you have to match the train's speed. Then, as you reach up and grab the rung on the ladder of the freight car you have to be prepared for a sudden "tug" as you're pulled aboard the train. Getting off of the train is also quite difficult. You have to be ready to run fast in the direction the train is moving the moment your feet hit the ground – otherwise you could easily tumble over and land under the trains' wheels.

    I had several bad experiences when I attempted to disembark from a moving train. On at least two occasions I tumbled as my feet hit the ground and almost rolled under the wheels. It was a very frightening experience. Those two incidents taught me to mend my ways – my days as a "junior hobo" were over.

The following three stories appeared during a five-week period in the fall of 1933 in the *Shenandoah Evening Herald*:

TAMAQUA BOY CRUSHED UNDER FREIGHT TRAIN

Ralph Albertson, 17-year-old Tamaqua High School student, was fatally injured last evening about 10:30 when his head was crushed and body badly mangled on the Reading Railroad near East Mahanoy Junction, Lakeside.

The wheels of a southbound freight train, which young Albertson attempted to board, crushed the youth's head, severed his left arm near the elbow, and tore off his right leg above the knee.

A companion, whose name was not learned, notified the telegraph operator at East Mahanoy Junction, who flagged a pusher engine, which took the youth's body to Lansford, where it was removed to the morgue.

The victim of the tragic accident is survived by his parents, three brothers and three sisters.

MAN IS GROUND TO DEATH UNDER WM. PENN TRAIN

Paul Buroznick, about 45, of Raven Run, was fatally injured about 8:15 o'clock last evening at Wm. Penn, when he is believed to have fallen beneath the wheels of a Reading coal train, which he attempted, to board while en route home. Both legs were so badly mangled that an emergency operation was required at the Locust Mountain State Hospital, here he died at 11:30 o'clock last night.

Buroznick was found lying along the railroad tracks by Michael Coyle of Wm. Penn, who, together with Roy Jones, also of that community, had the injured man removed to the hospital. An emergency operation was performed, the left leg being amputated above the knee and the right leg below the knee. Both limbs had almost been severed. The unfortunate man never regained consciousness after being admitted to the hospital, and consequently could not be questioned as to just how the accident occurred.

LOCAL BOY LOSES ARM RIDING FREIGHT TRAIN

Jumping from a freight car to a coal car near Park Place, about seven miles east of here, on a train which he boarded in Shenandoah, Alfred Gavrych, 12-year-old parochial school pupil of Shenandoah, suffered injuries which necessitated amputation of his left arm above the elbow, in an emergency operation performed at the Locust Mountain State Hospital late yesterday afternoon.

Young Gavrych son of Mr. and Mrs. Alex Gavrych is said to have boarded the Lehigh Valley Railroad train in Shenandoah "to go for a ride." Gavrych in attempting to jump from a boxcar to a coal car fell between the cars, his left arm being so badly mangled from the shoulder to the hand that amputation ten inches from the shoulder was necessary to save the youth's life.

The Ashland Daily News, August 1, 1934:

Lad, 9, Pulls
Cousin, 12, From
Underneath Train

An attempt to hop a freight train late yesterday will cost 12-year-old Jackie Willing of Seek, near Tamaqua, both his legs, if not his life.

The boy went swimming yesterday afternoon with a group of youthful companions in a "mud hole" at Red Ridge, between Tamaqua and Barnesville. After the lads finished swimming they began picking huckleberries near the Reading railway tracks north of Tamaqua.

When a freight appeared Jackie was determined to board it and ride to Tamaqua. But he failed in his effort and fell under the speeding train.

While car after car passed over Jackie's two crushed legs his cousin, John Willing, 9-years-old, of Tamaqua, crawled along the tracks on his stomach to reach Jackie's side. John had seen the accident. He noticed that Jackie's head and shoulders rested beyond the reach of the train's wheels.

John finally reached Jackie and pulled him away from the track. Portions of the boy's legs were left behind on the railway line.

The group of swimmers carried Jackie to the nearby state highway, hailed a passing car and had him removed to the Coaldale Hospital.

During the night two blood transfusions were given the lad so that his right leg could be amputated at the hip. A third blood transfusion was given this morning and physicians said if the boy rallies sufficiently they will amputate the left leg at the knee late today.

The accident occurred at 4:30 o'clock yesterday afternoon. Members of the crew in charge of the freight were unaware their train had run over the lad who had attempted to board it.

Jackie Willing is a son of Mr. and Mrs. Harold Willing of Seek. John Willing, the boy who rescued his cousin, is a son of Mr. and Mrs. Thomas Willing of Seek.

The *Shenandoah Evening Herald,* Nov. 30, 1935:

GIRL HAS LEFT LEG CUT OFF BY READING TRAIN

While playing on the Reading Railroad tracks south of town yesterday afternoon, Florence Yanonis, 12-year-old daughter of Mr. and Mrs. Frank Yanonis hopped a freight car, lost her footing, slipped under a wheel, and had her left leg amputated above the knee.

She is in the Locust Mountain State Hospital in a serious condition. Her family today stated that the girl left home about 3:00 o'clock with several boy and girl companions to play near the tracks.

Then it was learned that Florence and one or two of her friends hopped a slowly-moving freight train. Florence gave out a scream as she lost her grip and fell under the car. Before she was able to free her whole body, her leg was caught.

Florence is a fifth grade pupil at the North Union Street School. She has one sister, Jennie and two brothers, Frank and William.

The Bonus Army

In 1924, Congress approved the Bonus Bill, which provided compensation (in the form of bonus certificates) for veterans of World War I. The problem, however, was that the bonus certificates (like bonds) were not redeemable until 1945, some 27 years after the Armistice in 1918. The only exception: payment was made to a veteran's family if he died before then.

In the summer of 1932, about 20,000 unemployed World War I veterans traveled to the nation's Capitol seeking early payment of their bonus certificates (in *Nothing to Fear*, Adam Cohen wrote, "One-fourth of the nation's workforce was unemployed and *Fortune* magazine estimated that 27 million Americans were without a regular income."). The veterans, who were called the Bonus Army or the Bonus Expeditionary Force (BEF), camped out on the Anacosta Flats in Washington, D.C., not too far from the Capitol. The soldiers, and in some cases their families, built makeshift housing from whatever materials they could find. There was little food available and living conditions were terrible.

13. Bonus army campsite, 1932.

The economic situation in the country could not have been worse – it was in a deep depression. Unemployment had reached 25 percent and millions of Americans were destitute (one can only wonder how many veterans committed suicide so their families could collect the bonus).

Unfortunately, the Federal Government did not handle the problem very well. While the House of Representatives passed a bill approving the bonus payment to the veterans, the bill was defeated in the Senate. President Hoover also resisted the demand by the soldiers for an early bonus payment.

The veterans felt Hoover and his administration were ignoring them. It was a hot summer, the soldiers were destitute and tension was building on both sides. On July 20, 1932, the first skirmish broke out between the police and the veterans. The fighting, which was intense at times, resulted in the arrest and removal of several leaders of the marchers. Other skirmishes soon followed and more marchers were arrested and jailed. The police ordered the veterans to leave by 8 a.m. on July 28. Further violence ensued and a number of police and veterans were injured. Sadly, one soldier was killed in the scuffle that followed and another was injured and died later.

14. Bonus army shacks were burned.

President Hoover, fearing that the situation was getting out of hand, ordered the U.S. Army, commanded by Chief of Staff General Douglas MacArthur, to complete the evacuation of the Bonus Army from Washington, D.C.

Apparently, General MacArthur went beyond Hoover's order to clear out the bonus marchers. Late in the afternoon of July 28, MacArthur ordered Major George S. Patton and his cavalry soldiers along with federal troops to break-up and rout the veterans. MacArthur also ordered them to torch all of the shacks built by the soldiers. The army and police used tanks, tear gas and bayonets to drive the veterans from the area. There were no serious injuries during the final operation. The federal government unceremoniously routed the veterans and their families and the bonus march was ended. It was a dark day in the history of the United States.

15. General Douglas MacArthur and Major Dwight Eisenhower.

Headline from *The Washington Post,* July 29, 1932:

ONE SLAIN, 60 HURT AS TROOPS ROUT B.E.F. WITH GAS BOMBS AND FLAMES

In *New Deal or Raw Deal*, Burton W. Folsom, Jr. wrote:

. . . photos blanketed the country showing the fleeting vets under fire from their own government. It was an election year, and when Roosevelt, then the Democratic candidate, saw the pictures and news reports he reportedly told Felix Frankfurter, "Well Felix, this will elect me." [Frankfurter was a Harvard professor and later was an adviser to FDR when he became president.]

A certain Major Dwight D. Eisenhower was General MacArthur's aide at the time. It is fair to say, however, that Eisenhower felt that the Federal Government should have used fewer troops and tried to end the encampment in a less unruly manner. Patton called it the "most distasteful form of service," and later wrote on how such matters could be resolved with less bloodshed. The routing of the Bonus Army provided some of the most indelible images of the Great Depression.

When Roosevelt became president, he also opposed paying the bonuses early on two different occasions. Congress, however, rejected FDR's second veto, granting the veterans immediate payment of their much-needed bonuses. In January 1936, the bonus bill became law and the veterans of World War I finally collected their bonus money. The total money paid was $1.9 billion to 3.5 million World War I veterans.

The veterans of World War I were treated deplorably; the entire situation should have been handled in a more constructive manner. A partial payment could have been made to the veterans early in 1932, when they traveled to Washington, D.C., the remainder could have been paid later.

I am a disabled veteran of World War II. When I was discharged in the spring of 1946 I began receiving my monthly pension payment. In addition, I was able to earn a college education under the GI Bill of Rights without undue delay. The speedy payment of benefits to the millions of GIs in World War II most likely came about, in part, from the harsh lessons learned during the bonus march.

16. A migrant family living in a trailer.

Hoover's Last Months in Office

The *Shenandoah Evening Herald,* March 25, 1932:

EMERGENCY RELIEF FUNDS ARE DRAINED

Chicago, March 25. (U.P.) – Emergency relief funds in a score of metropolitan cities have been drained, and others soon will be, leaving hundreds of thousands of jobless and needy to shift for themselves – or trust to the kindness of a spring season expected to release them from a bondage of cold and suffering.

City after city reported in a United Press survey that terrific burdens have wiped out funds appropriated from state and city treasuries or raised by popular subscription.

Many cities planned new drives to replenish relief finances. Others in dull despair feared starvation and want will take toll in the homes of unfortunate citizens.

Weary relief workers confessed their problem became more acute each day. Several suggested federal intervention as a possible solution of what they called "the worst crisis in the history of America."

The *Shenandoah Evening Herald*, July 20, 1932:

COUNTY EXPENDS $1,500,000 FOR RELIEF

Pottsville, July 20 – At present, over $1,500,000 is being expended annually in the county for relief, ... and the greatest amount of this sum will have to be regarded as standard and will have to be met out of the taxes of the county. The county is not extending all of the money, at least one-third of this tremendous outlay being met by private charities such as local relief and church organizations

Although a recent cut of 48 percent was made in the Mothers' Assistance Fund, at least 150 families are still on the roll and a waiting list of several hundred more deserving and eligible families give a fair idea of conditions in the county.

17. Children living in a migration camp.

The *Shenandoah Evening Herald,* May 14, 1932:

GENERAL CIGAR CO. HAS CLOSED FACTORY

The management of the General Cigar Co. announced today that its factory, at 128 North White street, [in Shenandoah] "would be closed." . . . It is understood that the executive and office forces of the local factory are to be taken care of at other factories; some of these employees were being transferred to the Mount Carmel plant.

The employees have been working on a part-time basis for the past two years, and it is believed that decreased production due to a poor market resulted in economy and efficiency measures, which necessitated a shutdown of the local cigar factory. A. J. Neumann is manager of the local plant.

Under normal working conditions, the General Cigar Company employed three hundred girls, with an annual salary list of almost a quarter of a million dollars. During the past two years as a result of economic conditions throughout the country the factory was forced on a part-time basis, but despite this the factory payroll amounted to almost $185,000 annually.

The lease on the factory building held by the General Cigar Company does not expire until some time next year, and it is possible that the factory may be re-opened. This however, does not seem very probable, as the management stated that machinery and other equipment is being shifted to various other factories of the company.

The early 1930s was the beginning of a 10-year-long economic nightmare. From a September 1929 high of 381, the Dow dropped to 41 in July 1932, a staggering 89 percent decline. In September 1931, unemployment was 17 percent; it continued to rise to an incredible high of 25 percent by early 1933. The economic contraction from 1929 to 1933 was arguably the most severe in U.S. History. In *The Hungry Years*, T.H. Watkins pointed out that in February 1933, there were 4.7 million families representing 18.6 million people who were receiving some form of relief – almost 15 percent of all Americans.

18. Migrant cotton pickers eating lunch.

The *Shenandoah Evening Herald,* May 31, 1932:

BLEW OFF HIS HEAD WITH DYNAMITE

Despondent for some time because he was unemployed, Frank Litawa, 45, a miner, took his life about 3:50 o'clock yesterday afternoon, when he blew off his head with a stick of dynamite.

Discovery of the suicide was made by Frank Liepiec, a neighbor, who heard the detonation, which took place in a wood shanty to the rear of the Litawa home. Sergeant Peter Wallace, of the local police department, and deputy Coroner Joseph Popalis were summoned. The deputy coroner announced that Litawa had been decapitated by the explosion, his right fore finger and right index finger [sic] also being blown off, making it apparent that Litawa had held the stick of dynamite to his head.

Surviving is his widow and one daughter, Mary.

The following two articles appeared during the month of October 1934 in the *Shenandoah Evening Herald*:

FRACKVILLE MINER BLOWS HIS HEAD OFF

Frank Debuaka, 47, Frackville, was found with his head blown off in a gangway of the Reppelier colliery, near Saint Clair, late yesterday afternoon. According to County Detective D. Buono and Deputy Coroner Thorn of St. Clair, who conducted an investigation, Debuaka took his life by tying a stick of dynamite around his head and then firing the explosive.

Surviving is his widow and six children, Anna, Catherine, Helen, Mildred, Mary and Frank Jr.

JOBLESS MAN BLOWS OFF HEAD WITH DYNAMITE

Albert Birkner, 56, unemployed miner, Mahanoy City, blew the back of his head away with dynamite Saturday evening about 9:30 o'clock. The suicide was found in the cellar of his home by his wife, who survives with seven children.

Birkner, unemployed for the past four years, is said to have been in ill health.

The *Shenandoah Evening Herald*, June 29, 1933:

MAN KILLS TWO CHILDREN AND SHOOTS TWO OTHERS

Muskogee, Okla. June 29 (U.P.) – Jap Ingram, a factory worker, was held today while authorities sought to determine why he shot and killed his infant son and 4-year-old daughter, and wounded two other relatives.

Ingram's only explanation of the shooting, officers said, was that he would "rather see my children dead than starving." He and his wife had been separated a week.

The shooting was at the rural home of Ingram's father-in-law, Sam Sewell. Witnesses said Ingram stood his baby son, Donald, and his daughter, Mary Lou, before him and said he was going to kill them.

Sewell ran to get a gun and was shot in the abdomen. John Doss, Sewell's stepson, was shot in the neck.

19. A youngster cooling off.

In December 2008, unemployment was 7.2 percent. It was 8.5 percent in March and went to 9.4 percent in May and continued to rise to 10.2 percent in October 2009 – the highest in 26 years – with over 16 million unemployed. In 1983, unemployment was over 10 percent. When unemployment figures reach close to double digits, comparisons are made to the days of the Great Depression (some analysts feel that because of the way current unemployment figures are calculated, that they should be higher when comparing them with data from the Depression).

Franklin Delano Roosevelt Becomes President

In *American-Made*, Nick Taylor wrote:

When Franklin D. Roosevelt took office as president of the United States in March 1933, as many as 15 million people – a quarter of the nation's workers – had no jobs and no hope of finding one. Factoring in their families, this meant that in a nation of 130 million, perhaps 60 million were literally without support: no money for rent, no food to feed their children, no coats against the wintry cold. Factories lay idle, storefronts vacant, fields plowed under. State governments, cities, and towns had exhausted their meager relief funds.

One of the earliest news events I remember was listening to our neighbor's radio when FDR was elected our 32nd president. The next day, I saw the huge headline about the landslide election in our neighbor's newspaper. I was 8 years old.

The New York Times (which cost 2 cents):

ROOSEVELT WINNER IN LANDSLIDE!

The results of the Nov. 8, 1932, presidential election: FDR won the popular vote 22,821,277 to Herbert Hoover's 15,761,254. The electoral count was: Roosevelt 472 and Hoover 59 (Pennsylvania, my home state, voted for Hoover).

20. Herbert Hoover and Franklin Roosevelt, 1933 inauguration.

In the presidential campaign, FDR raised the nation's hopes that things would soon get better. Though copyrighted in 1929, his campaign song, "Happy Days Are Here Again," was meant to reflect a new optimism. You can hear the snappy tune on YouTube online. The first three stanzas go like this:

So long sad times
Go long bad times
We are rid of you at last

Howdy gay times
Cloudy gray times
You are now a thing of the past

Happy days are here again
The skies above are clear again
So let's sing a song of cheer again
Happy days are here again

    FDR was inaugurated on March 4, 1933. It was in that first inauguration address that FDR delivered his famous line:

"The only thing we have to fear is fear itself."

In *Nothing to Fear*, Adam Cohen wrote:

> Roosevelt left the inaugural parade at dusk and made his way up to the Oval Room on the second floor. He had quietly arranged for the Senate to confirm his Cabinet that afternoon, [Inauguration Day] and now he was about to do something that had never been done before: swearing in a full Cabinet at once. The incoming Cabinet members had been summoned to appear [at the Oval Room] but they had not been told why.
>
>   Roosevelt announced to the Cabinet that Justice [Benjamin] Cardozo would be swearing them in. . . . As each stepped forward, the silver-haired Justice Cardozo administered the oath of

office and Roosevelt extended a congratulatory handshake and a signed commission.

21. A bread line in New York City.

When FDR became president, the country was deeply troubled. No one could get a bank loan. Employment was 25 percent (an all-time high) and the farming industry was in shambles because demand for agricultural goods was down. On March 9, FDR sent to Congress the Emergency Banking Act that was drafted in large part by Hoover's Administration; the act was passed and signed into law in the same day, according to Adam Cohen.

While Roosevelt had many important issues to deal with, none loomed larger than the banking crisis. It was the one he would address first, since more than 4,000 banks had gone under in the first 60 days of 1933.

Adam Cohen wrote:

> On Sunday evening, March 12, [1933], Roosevelt addressed the nation. "The President wants to come into your home and sit beside your fireside for a little fireside chat," the announcer said, and an institution was born. Roosevelt described the banking crisis in calmly reassuring tones to an estimated 60 million people gathered around their radio consoles.

That first fireside chat, only 15 minutes long, was hugely successful and a confidence builder for the nation. It was a breakthrough in presidential communication. The Emergency Banking Act of 1933 was FDR's first victory. Will Rogers, the most famous humorist of his day, said FDR made everyone understand it, even the bankers.

There was no TV, and many families did not have radios in the early 1930s. Many could not even afford newspapers, so it was difficult to follow what was happening to the economy on a daily basis. For those who had access to a radio, FDR's informal radio addresses were very popular. It was President Roosevelt's way of personally talking to the American people about hard times the country faced and what he was trying to do to get America back on track again. FDR gave 30 evening speeches – "chats" – over 10 years. Roosevelt had a great tenor voice and was indeed eloquent on the radio.

The *Shenandoah Evening Herald,* March 22, 1933:

3,000 FAMILIES AIDED BY LOCAL RED CROSS

The following detailed report of the activities of the Shenandoah Chapter, American Red Cross, during the four months' period from Nov. 1, 1932, when the first allotment of cotton material was received from the national headquarters, to March 5, this year, will give an idea of the work accomplished in distributing clothing and dress material to needy families in the area.

Nearly 3,000 families are listed with the chapter, and in many cases the families are altogether destitute, requiring clothing of all kinds for practically every member, from the head of the family to the smallest child.

This service is all the more valuable when it is remembered that, at no time during the months past, has the work of checking and distributing goods and material, been other than voluntary. This is also so in reference to the issue of Red Cross flour, which is given out on an average of 189,303 pounds monthly.

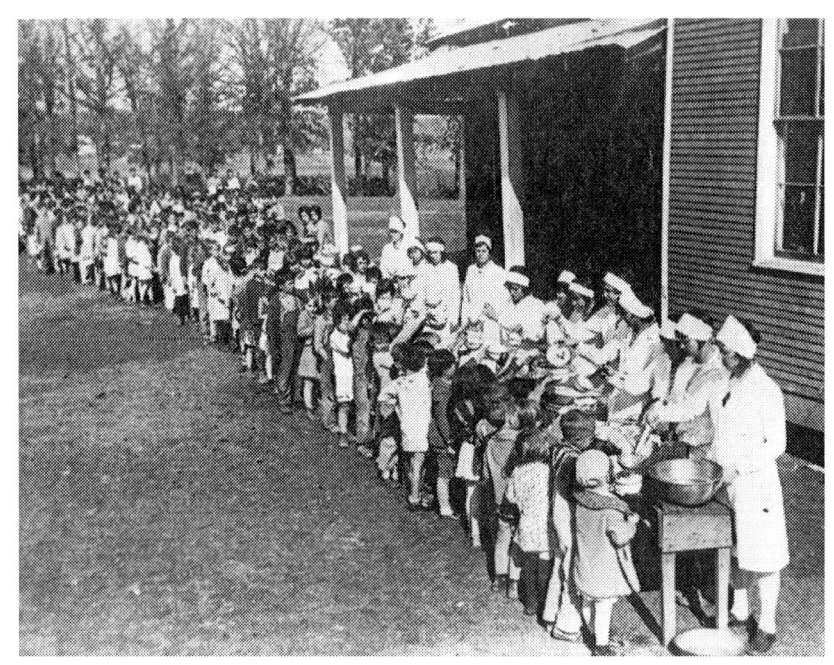

22. Children in a soup line.

The *Shenandoah Evening Herald,* May 16, 1933:

WM. PENN COLLIERY CLOSES INDEFINITELY

Officials of the Susquehanna Collieries Company, operators of the Wm. Penn colliery, announced today that "on account of market conditions, Wm. Penn colliery will remain idle for an indefinite period" and all employees are requested to remove their tools.

The market for anthracite coal is very slow at the present time, as the large buyers have withheld the usual spring orders due to an anticipated reduction in the price of hard coal, the possibility of further wage negotiations, and the uncertainty of the economic situation.

Edward W. Williams, Shamokin, is superintendent of the Susquehanna Collieries Company and C. F. Grum, assistant superintendent of the Wm. Penn colliery.

Approximately 450 men will be placed on the unemployed list as a result of the colliery being temporarily placed out of operation.

The Ashland Daily News, Sept. 12, 1933:

Schuylkill One of Two Counties Where 40 Percent are Idle

Harrisburg, Pa. (UP) – Employment in Pennsylvania, for the fifth consecutive month, showed a gain, the Department of Labor and Industry reported today. The gain affected all the major industries in the state except the transportation group.

Schuylkill and Carbon counties are the only two where unemployment is estimated at more than 40 per cent of the working population. Five months ago there were six counties in this group.

The *Shenandoah Evening Herald*, Sept. 19, 1933:

50,000 MINERS PLAN TO MARCH ON WASHINGTON

Tamaqua, Pa., Sept. 19. (U.P.) – A march of 50,000 unemployed anthracite miners to Washington to demand equalization of work in the hard coal fields was being planned today by the idle men of the Panther Creek Valley section.

The march is scheduled to take place when the anthracite coal code comes before the National Recovery Administration for a hearing. The demonstration is to demand that work be spread among the 130,000 hard coal diggers instead of allowing some collieries to remain idle.

Organizers for the demonstration were sent into the Mahanoy City, Shenandoah, Pittston, Wilkes-Barre, Scranton, Shamokin, Mt. Carmel, Hazleton and Pittston districts today to arouse enthusiasm for the "parade to Washington."

The men, many of whom have been idle from one to five years, are becoming restless.

The *Shenandoah Evening Herald*, Nov. 28, 1933:

12,000 TONS OF BOOTLEG COAL IN PHILLY WEEKLY

Philadelphia, Nov. 28. (U.P.) – More than 12,000 tons of "bootleg" coal are being brought to this city each week by itinerant dealers operating 2,540 trucks, according to a survey made by the Philadelphia Retail Coal Conference.

A similar survey a year ago revealed that 3,000 tons of "bootleg" coal was being brought into the city each week.

"Bootleg" coal is that mined at isolated workings in the anthracite region by individuals who attempt to market it in competition with coal companies. Yesterday five dealers were convicted and fined on charges of giving short weights in their sales.

"The prevailing method of determining weight seems to be haphazard by count of the shovelfuls unloaded at any given point. Another method has been to use two sizes of canvas bags."

The Ashland Daily News, Sept. 13, 1933:

Stiff Sentence Is Given to Ashland Lads For Station Robbery

Judge Hicks handed down a stiff sentence to four Ashland youths. William Cress, Charles Garboski, Walter Dunleavy and Edward Warbet, who were convicted of robbing the Reading passenger station at Gordon. They got but 18 cents for their trouble and drew a sentence of from 1 1/2 to three years in prison and in addition were sentenced to pay costs of prosecution, a fine of $1 and to restore the stolen money.

The Ashland Daily News, March 9, 1934:

Get 3 Years for Theft of 3 Cents at Gordon Station

Charged with having broken into the Reading station at Gordon last year Harold Shipp, of Locust Gap and Thomas Schaeffer, of Locust Dale, today pleaded guilty in court at Pottsville before Judge C. M. Palmer.

The youths were sentenced to serve from three to six years in the county prison, to pay a fine of $5 each, and to pay the costs of the prosecution.

The youths got three cents in cash and a rack of 3,489 tickets in their robbery at Gordon and railway police worked for several weeks until they tracked them down and made the arrests.

F. Stokes, head of the railway police, appeared before court at Pottsville today as the prosecutor in the case.

Our Boarder Mike

When I was about 5 years old we had a boarder, named Mike Romanskevitz, who was Russian. Mike was a coal miner who did not have a family, and since he was a source of income my Mom took him in. Mike boarded with us for several years; we also had other boarders from time to time. It was not unusual for families in the Coal Region to take in boarders because they provided much-needed income.

In a picture taken in front of our home, Mike is holding our dog, Tiny. Note my bare feet – the little girl is Margie Colahan, our neighbor. I believe that our family car, shown in the picture, was a mid-1920s Whippet.

23. Margie Colahan, Mike Romaskevitz and Harry Bobonich

Mike was a World War I veteran who served in the U.S. Army. He was a big man who was badly burned while fighting with the American troops in Europe. I can still recall his web-like hands. They were scarred, unsightly and he was unable to squeeze his hands together to make a tight fist.

As Mike grew older and was unemployed, he spent more time at the Veteran's Hospital in Bath, N.Y. After his last visit with us, that is where I took him. Later on, when I visited him at the hospital, I realized that his health was seriously deteriorating. Not long after my last visit I received notice that he had passed away. Sadly, he was just one of many homeless soldiers, who simply pass away, quietly and all alone.

On Relief

24. Woman waiting for the relief agent.

In May 1933 FDR continued federal relief (started under Hoover) when Congress passed the Federal Emergency Relief Fund Act (FERA) with $500 million to aid the unemployed and starving.

Our family was on relief during the early days of the Depression. The amount of food given to a family was limited, and the relief food was only provided for a certain length of time. I recall one afternoon when we received a box of groceries from the relief agency. I was eager to see what was in the box; we began to take out the groceries and place them on the kitchen table.

Some of the food came in small boxes or packages labeled "not to be sold." They were items like raisins, prunes and flour. Since the labels were removed from the canned goods, we didn't know what any particular can contained. As it turned out, most of the unlabeled cans contained vegetables. At first, I was a little disappointed because I was hoping for more peaches, cherries or pears.

The *Shenandoah Evening Herald*, Dec. 12, 1933:

Schools Close, Cut Terms; Teachers Unpaid, Jobless, As Depression Continues

By Frederick C. Othman
United Press Staff Correspondent

Washington, Dec. 12. (U.P.) – Almost from one end of the nation to the other, education of America's 28 million school children has suffered severely from the depression.

Information at the office of George F. Zook, Commissioner of Education, indicates that some of the greatest difficulties have been in the Deep South, where many counties are reported without normal school facilities. More normal are the Far West, the states around the Great Lakes and New England.

Zook's information indicated that virtually all of the 575,000 school children in Alabama, for instance, have been affected by shortened terms, and that conditions might be made even more difficult next year.

It was pointed out here that relief might come from the Civil Works Administration, but red tape specifies that the CWA can hire none of its $15 a week workers, except from the relief rolls. Teachers in Alabama and elsewhere have been too proud to affix their names to charity lists, it was said.

The *Ashland Daily News,* Dec. 27, 1933:

Every 20th Person in U.S. Is Now on Federal Payroll

By Frederick C. Othman

Washington, D.C., (UP) – More than 6,000,000 men and women now are on Uncle Sam's payroll.

One out of every 20 persons in the country has a federal position of one kind or another. Never before in peacetime has the percentage been so high.

The *Shenandoah Evening Herald,* March 1, 1934:

SCHUYLKILL CO. GETS $159,503 FOR RELIEF

March Allocation Also Includes
$2,040 More for Fuel,
$50,000 Extra for Food.

TWO MILLION DOLLARS FOR CLOTHES

The *Shenandoah Evening Herald*, April 13, 1934:

4,700,000 FAMILIES ON RELIEF

Washington, April 13, (U.P.) – Relief rolls reached an all-time peak of 4,700,000 families April, 1934, despite employment increases, Relief Administrator Harry L. Hopkins said today.

Hopkins attributed the increase to rapid exhaustion of monetary reserves of persons who had been unemployed during the major portion of the depression.

The 4,700,000 figure, Hopkins said, is equal to approximately 18,000,000 persons.

25. A sharecropper's daughter.

The *Shenandoah Evening Herald*, Oct. 23, 1934:

DISTRESSED FAMILIES NEED STOVES, BEDDING

An appeal for two families in dire circumstances is made today by Captain John Berkhoudt of the Salvation Army. Both families are in need of cook stoves, and anyone having such equipment, which they are going to discard, is asked to communicate with the captain at the Army headquarters on East Lloyd street.

One family living on East Centre Street, with nine children, had neither a cook nor heating stove. Captain Berkhoudt states that there are no mattresses in the home and the children are sleeping on paper.

At a home on West Coal Street, a cook stove is also badly needed by a poverty-stricken family with four children.

The *Shenandoah Evening Herald*, Oct. 9, 1934:

FIVE FATHERS BESIEGE RELIEF HEADQUARTERS

McKees Rocks, Pa., Oct. 9 (U.P.) – The siege of McKees Rocks relief headquarters by five men demanding shoes and clothing to enable their children to go to school continued today.

"I've had to keep my kids out of school for three weeks," said Joseph Dudak, "and I'm going to stay here until I get some clothes for them."

Dudack's four companions supported him. The five are fathers of a total of 17 children.

They were bearded and hollow-eyed when dawn awoke them this morning in the chairs where they had slept all night. They began their vigil, one at a time, yesterday and all the pleas and threats of relief officials failed to budge them.

Relief workers called police when the fifth man came in asked for shoes and clothing, was refused, and sat down in a chair.

"We're being threatened by radicals," they telephoned the police. "Send some officers up right way."

Police Chief Michael Matsey went to the relief offices in the first National Bank Building.

"We don't mean no trouble," one of them told Chief Matsey. "All we want is clothes and shoes for our children. We wait until we get them."

Chief Matsey refused to throw them out.

"I know these men," he told the relief workers. "They are all honest citizens. They work whenever they can get work."

When relief workers went home last night, they left the five men sitting in the office. When they returned to work this morning, the five men were still there.

"They told us," said Andrew Barrett, one of the besiegers, "that we could stay here until 8 a.m. or 8 p.m., and we wouldn't get anything. They wouldn't tell us why."

Relief workers refused to tell reporters why they would not issue clothing and shoes to the five.

Besides Dudack, who is father of three children, and Barrett, father of four, the besiegers are Albert Hogan, father of six; E. Hanna, father of two, and Frank Hamilton, father of two.

Bargains Everywhere

It wasn't a problem that prices were too high – many people didn't have enough money to buy even the cheapest things. An adult who found a penny on the street during the Depression would pick it up.

During those difficult times, you could buy an orange for 2 cents. And if you had 3 cents, you could buy two bananas or *The New York Times*; everyone in Big Mine Run would have bought the bananas in lieu of the newspaper. A pound of sugar was 4 cents and a cup of coffee cost a nickel. An ice cream cone cost 5 cents; however, if you were kid you didn't have a nickel. Five cents would also buy two bars of soap.

A can of pork and beans went for 8 cents and if you had another penny, you could buy a box of raisins. And all kids agreed that that the best buy of all was a ticket to see a cowboy movie, which cost a dime.

A pound of chicken or hamburger cost 12 cents, and you could buy a quart of milk for 14 cents. A pack of cigarettes cost 15 cents, and a single cigarette cost a penny. A gallon of gasoline cost about 16 cents. If you had 17 cents, you could purchase a dozen eggs, or a pound of baloney or a pound of cheese. A pound of steak or a pound of coffee cost 19 cents. For that same amount of money, you could get a lunch, which consisted of carrots, onions, a slice of bread and half an apple. If you had a quarter, you could get two eggs, toast, coffee and a small piece of apple pie. On the other hand, a Mom could feed her family for a quarter. She would buy a can of Campbell's pork and beans, add water and ketchup and maybe add a little molasses.

A girls' work dress cost 45 cents. A pair of summer shoes (we called them sneakers) was 90 cents, but a pair of year-round shoes cost $2.

If you wanted to eat at a hotel and order an expensive dinner like lobster, it would cost $2.50. A ticket for the first game of the 1934 World Series between the Detroit Tigers and the St. Louis Cardinals cost $3.30. An ordinary automobile tire was $3.95. A Tudor Ford with a V-8 engine cost $450. In 1935 my Uncle Bill purchased a Chevrolet coupe for $650. But for many people even the lowest prices were not low enough.

My Mom was always thinking about her family. She took out a life insurance policy on my Dad, just in case. The insurance man's name was Mr. Farrell (somehow I still remember his name) and he came every two weeks to collect the insurance payment, which was 10 cents. He had a leather case about the size and shape of a loaf of bread. He would sit down and dutifully open it up and record payment of my Mom's 10 cents. Sometimes she didn't have the dime, but he was always pleasant. She would usually give Mr. Farrell a small glass of homemade wine when she didn't have the money. And so, the last item in this list of "bargains" is that for a dime you could purchase a life insurance policy – sort of.

It is of interest to note that in the America of 1935, the average income per person was only about $400. The average middle-class family earned $1,348, each year.

26. A family on the move.

The Ashland Daily News, June 7, 1935:

5 Are Executed in 2 States, Mother and Son Hanged

By UNITED PRESS

Two states conducted mass executions today.

Delaware exacted the extreme penalty from a mother and her son – May Carey, 55, and Howard Carey, 27. They killed Mrs. Carey's brother.

Massachusetts executed Murton and Irving Millen and Abraham Faber. They killed four men in a series of robberies.

By Joseph S. Wasney

Georgetown, Del. (UP) – A Mother and her son were executed on the same gallows at dawn today.

They were: Mrs. May H. Carey, 55; and her eldest son, Howard, 27. They murdered Mrs. Carey's brother, Robert R. Hutchins, for his insurance. Another of her sons James 23, is serving life. He was an accomplice. Her third son, Lawrence, 21, is in jail for burglary.

The executions took place in the yard of Sussex County prison where Lawrence is confined.

From the trap, Mrs. Carey called out in a loud voice:

"My way is clear. I have nothing else to say."

The mask was tied over her face, the noose adjusted, and at 5:07 a.m. EST the trap dropped. Seventeen minutes later she was pronounced dead.

Like his mother, Howard mounted the 13 gallows steps without assistance. On the trap, he licked his lips and said in a trembling voice:

"What I did was against my will. I feel anyone in my place would have done the same thing. I hope to see my little ones on the other side."

He mumbled a prayer while the hangman's assistant waited, the death mask in his hand. Howard finished, the mask was tied across his face, and at 5:41 a.m. he dropped. He was pronounced dead at 6:08.

Howard leaves a wife and three children.

State Prison, Charlestown, Mass. (UP) – Three murderers were executed in the electric chair early today. They were the brothers, Millen – Murton, 35, and Irving, 22 – and Abraham Faber 25.

Making Do

My Dad did not work very much during the entire Depression, so we had no regular income for some period of time. As a kid, I realized we didn't have much, but I didn't know that we were dirt-poor. We got along with very little because we had to. It didn't take me long to understand that "making do" often meant "doing without."

Some of my clothes were hand-me-downs from friends or relatives since I didn't have any brothers (I did have three older sisters). When my parents did buy a jacket or coat for me, it was always a little too large. I was told that I would grow into it, but by the time I had, the darn thing was almost worn out. On holidays, it was not unusual to see some kids all dressed up in hand-me-downs.

I was also given a pair of second-hand shoes that were too large for me – I wore those out too. During the summer in Big Mine Run, most kids didn't need any shoes – we ran around barefoot, and as youngster, I didn't go to a barber. Someone in my family cut my hair or sometimes the lady next door cut it for no charge.

27. Mother with her two children.

Practically all the boys in Big Mine Run went to grade school in overalls, which were loose-fitting coarse trousers with a bib front and shoulder straps. Many had sewn patches on them. Some of the kids (not all) were embarrassed to wear patched overalls. Today boys and girls in high school and college prefer to wear patched blue jeans, which came later. Ironically, there aren't any holes under those patches.

Many women practiced small economics, but they didn't call it that – it was making do. Cutting down old, worn adult clothing to fit younger children was a common practice. Summer coats were often lined with older material for the winter. If a mother only had $5 a week, she would somehow find a way to feed her family of six – stale bread at the right price was all right.

Fred Baldino, a decorated paratrooper in the 82nd Airborne Division in World War II, also grew up in Big Mine Run during the Depression. Fred was reared in a family of 12 – seven other brothers and four sisters. Fred was quick to point out that since he was one of the younger brothers, he was given many hand-me-downs while growing up (Fred presently lives in Burbank, Calif., with his wife Mary).

If young people complained too much, they were quickly reminded of the following saying:

USE IT UP
WEAR IT OUT
MAKE IT DO
OR DO WITHOUT

It was not unusual for kids to go without warm clothing during the winter. My friend, Richard Kerr Sr., from Clearfield, Pa., also remembers those difficult times. He said he could recall a young child coming to school in just a shirt – no jacket – in the middle of the winter.

28. Family living in a temporary home.

There were times when a sharp nail protruded up from the heel of my shoe and "into the heel of my foot." I would hobble along for a while. Eventually I would stop, take off my shoe and flatten down the pointed nail with a small rock. Sometimes I would put a small piece of paper or even a leaf over the nail. Then I put my shoe back on and continued on my way, walking more comfortably. When I got home I would pound the small nail down some more.

Sometimes our parents bought soles and heels to mend our worn-out shoes. We had a two-foot high iron pedestal shaped like a human foot called a "last" that we used to repair our shoes. The worn-out shoe was placed upside-down on the last and the new heel was nailed on. Then we glued on the sole. After a while the soles came unglued at the toes and I made a noisy flapping sound as I walked.

Stephanie Misner, who lives in Shippensburg, Pa., told me that her grandmother, Louise Anzalone, who lived in Yatesboro, Pa., would unravel a sweater when it was too small for any of her children to wear. She would use the wool to make another useful garment.

Shirley, a friend who asked that I not use her last name, grew up during the Depression on a farm in Iowa. She recalled working with her mother, Opal, and her sister to make "feed sack dresses" from cloth grain bags. It took two bags to make one dress. The sacks had a flowery pattern on them, which gave the dresses a "little feminine touch."

As they were browsing about the store, Opal reminded her daughters that they only had one empty feed sack at home and if they couldn't find that same pattern on another, they would have to look for two other sacks with a matching pattern.

Mary Mowery, library technician at Shippensburg University, said her great Aunt, Ethel Crider, of Newburg, Pa., also used feed sacks to make dresses for young girls. When the feed companies changed the sacks to plain burlap bags, Ethel was disappointed.

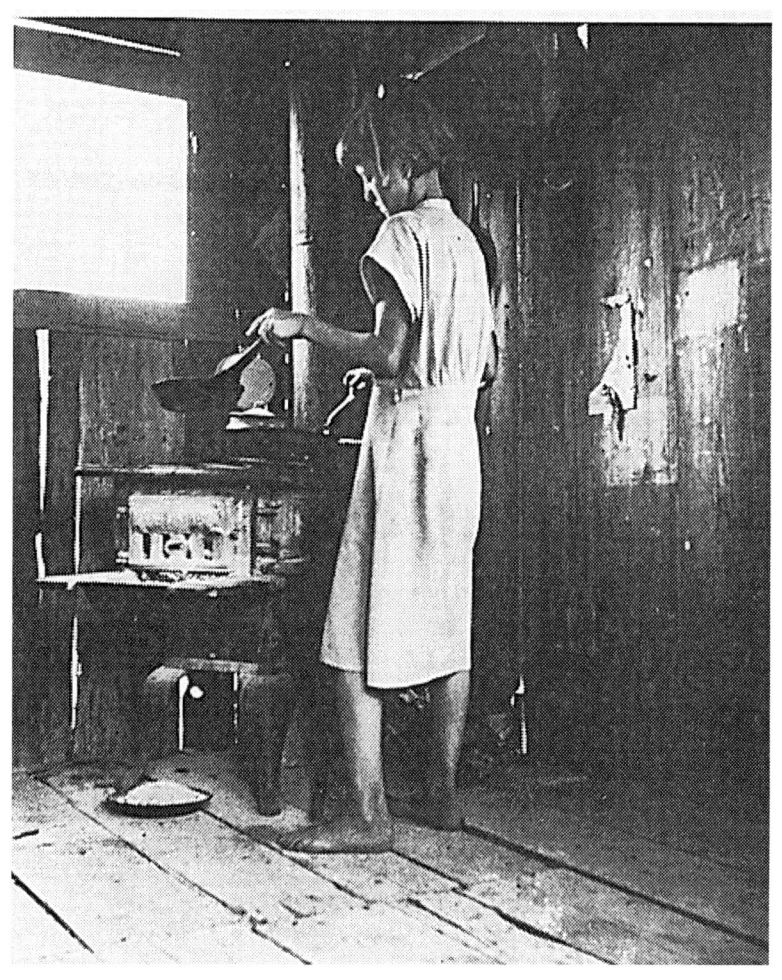

29. A girl making supper, 1936.

Some families used 100-pound sugar and flour bags to make dresses. Whenever a hem was dropped, the thread was always saved. You know, it might come in handy somewhere.

Joseph McAndrew, who lives in Hummelstown, Pa., related this story from his mother, Elizabeth Teeple. Elizabeth, who was reared in Carbondale, Pa., said her father worked on the railroad during the Great Depression and supported a family of 10, which was not easy, though anyone who had a job during those times, however difficult, had it much better than someone who was unemployed. If one had a job during the Depression, it wasn't the worst of times.

There was a period of time when we had no electricity. I read and did my homework by the light of a kerosene lamp. And when we finally did get electric lights, I quickly learned to turn off the light whenever I left a room. I was taught to save, even if it was only a penny. To this day, some seven decades later, I still turn off the lights when I go from one room to another. Those old habits of not wasting money die very slowly.

Simply put, it was a matter of just making do and also hoping that some day soon the economic situation would get a little better. People were, in a way, compelled to be self-sufficient. They also learned to be self-reliant and gained a knack for turning nothing into something. If something broke, you tried to fix it somehow. There was no throwing it out and buying a new one. Making do became way of life. Generally speaking, people did not expect too much.

The Ashland Daily News, July 23, 1935:

Half-Cent Pieces May Be Coined in a Few Weeks

Washington, D.C. (UP) – Price tags on thousands of items in every day use may soon be in fractions of a cent under a proposal bearing approval of the treasury.

Issuance of new one-half cent pieces for the first time in the United States since 1857, when 35,180 were minted, is proposed in a plan which Secretary of the Treasury Henry Morgenthau, Jr., will offer to Congress.

The new coins, if approved by Congress, might also bring a new metal in circulation as legal tender. It was indicated that they may be made in bronze or an aluminum alloy. They may be in circulation within a few weeks.

Approval of the new coins was given in response to appeals from states having sales taxes. At least 16 states have straight percentage sales taxes averaging about two percent on all purchases. Thus a 25-cent purchase would call for an additional ½ cent sales tax payment.

The *Shenandoah Evening Herald*, Oct. 17, 1935:

Price of Bread Increased Cent A Loaf Here: Bakers Blame High Cost Of Flour

Bakeries serving Shenandoah raised the price of bread one cent a loaf yesterday, bringing the price here up to the level prevailing generally in this section this week.

Other baked goods were not increased, merchants said. Most bread is now selling at 11 cents, although a few brands and grades are 12 and 13 cents.

The price increase is nation-wide. Leaders of bakers' organizations say some of their members have been forced into bankruptcy in attempting to absorb the costs themselves.

The new burden on consumers at this rate of increase was roughly figured at more than $100,000,000 a year.

30. A dust bowl family moving west.

Dynamite (duley) Boxes

In Big Mine Run, everyone knew that "a stick of duley" meant "a stick of dynamite." Each stick was about eight inches long and the diameter of an ordinary household broom handle.

I was quite young when my father would bring home empty duley boxes from the colliery where he worked. A duley box, which contained 24 sticks of dynamite, was about the size of a modern microwave oven.

The box was made from quality pinewood. The four sides were held together with tight V-shaped joints (no nails). In the early 1930s we moved into a home owned by the coal company. Since we didn't have much furniture, we used the duley boxes as stools, chairs, small tables and storage containers. I often played with them – it was easy to stack the boxes on top of one another. They were easy to take apart and my father used them to build other furniture, shelves and even some wooden toys.

Pack Rats

Many survivors of the depression became pack rats as a matter of necessity. Every scrap of cloth or twine was saved. In fact, we saved practically everything. People couldn't bear to part with anything of potential value, and that was everything. We focused on needs and not wants.

Even when things were a little better economically, someone would say to my Mom, "Why are you saving this or that?" Her response was, "I dunno for sure, but I know I'm gonna use it for somethin'."

Saving this and saving that became a habit; it was a lesson we learned well. Generally speaking, I think people felt that the lessons learned during the Depression served them well later. In many ways our personalities were shaped during those hard times, and we carried those habits with us into the 21st century. Frugality and survival went together.

To this day, I still do not squander anything. I'm sure there were times when our two children, Chris and Greg, thought I was too thrifty – or better, too stingy.

Layaway Plan

Layaway was a procedure for buying retail goods that enabled customers to put an item on reserve and make payments on it until it was paid in full. Layaway rose to popularity during the Depression when most shoppers didn't have enough money to pay for an item all at once. I recall Mom making small payments for items she was purchasing on layaway. It was a method of buying that helped shoppers get merchandise they wanted without going into debt.

Unlike credit cards, layaway procedures did not charge interest nor require a good credit rating. Layaway was popular for about 50 years – until the 1980s. Retailers discontinued layaway buying when shoppers began to have access to easy credit using the very convenient "credit card."

Christmas Clubs were another type of layaway plan that was popular, which was started by banks. A customer invested a small amount of money in a bank account each week at the beginning of the year. The bank would accept even a dime or a quarter, or whatever you could afford to invest weekly. At the end of the year the bank returned the amount invested and the customer had money to spend for Christmas shopping. After my sisters began working, they participated in Christmas Clubs, but the amount they invested weekly was 10 or 25 cents.

Bartering

One day when I was quite young, I saw a farmer and another man trade a sack of potatoes for a bag of coal. It was the first time I saw two adults barter. Subsequently, I noticed that the farmer who came to Woodland Heights selling his produce often had a bag of coal or two on his truck. I knew that he had just made a trade down the road somewhere. While I was curious and surprised to see adults engage in barter, it was a common practice in the Coal Region during the Depression.

Many times people didn't have enough money to pay the doctor when he made a house call. The fee was usually $1, but that was a dollar more than some could afford. It was not unusual for someone to give a doctor a chicken or some vegetables as payment.

A chicken farmer who needed feed for his flock might have exchanged eggs or chickens with another farmer who had an excess of wheat or corn. A farmer who raised pigs could trade bacon or ham for fruit from someone who had an orchard, and a dairy farmer might exchange milk or butter for grain products to feed his cows. People not only bartered for food, clothing and even housing, but also for other services.

My father was a great mushroom picker, and when he took a bucket full of mushrooms for my Uncle Bill Kuschick in Frackville – who loved mushrooms – he would give my father a quart of whiskey.

On the lighter side of things, we kids also traded one thing for another – we traded all sorts of worthless things. We didn't know we were bartering–we just called it "swapping." You know, "wanna swap this for that?" We would often shake hands to seal the deal, and sometimes if a kid felt that he got a good deal, he'd say "Touch black – never get it back," and he would race to touch something black.

FDR's First 100 Days

31. A long line of jobless men in Camden, N. J. (ca.1935).

The timely theme of FDR's inaugural address was:

"Action, and action now."

In *Nothing to Fear*, Adam Cohen wrote:

Roosevelt's distinctive leadership style meant that his inner circle had enormous influence – and a rare chance to shape history. Five of Roosevelt's advisers – Raymond Moley, Lewis Douglas, Henry Wallace Frances Perkins, and Harry Hopkins – had the greatest impact on the

Hundred Days. They did not have the biggest titles in the administration, although Perkins and Wallace were cabinet members. They were simply the people who, by virtue of their jobs, talents, rapport with the president, and force of personality, were able to leave the greatest mark.

In Roosevelt's first hundred days in office, he was able to get 15 major pieces of legislation passed. The bills, which addressed everything from banking and industry to agriculture and social welfare, passed quickly as Congress attempted to reshape the economy. It was a series of unprecedented legislative reforms. It was also the beginning of large-scale deficit spending to fund federal relief efforts for a nation in crisis. All future presidents have been measured against FDR's first hundred days in office.

The Civilian Conservation Corps (CCC)

About 1.5 million people were unemployed in 1929; by 1931 that number had increased to eight million. In 1933, unemployment reached a staggering 12.8 million. Unemployment was at 25 percent – an all-time high. FDR clearly had to address the problem. In his inaugural address, Roosevelt said, "our greatest primary task is to put people to work."

In March 1933, FDR signed the bill establishing the Civilian Conservation Corps (CCC). It was one of his early reform programs, designed to provide work opportunities for young, unmarried men between 18 and 25 years of age. They enlisted for a six-month period and could reenlist three more times, for a total of two years. The program, which was run in semi-military style and administered by the U.S. Army, enrolled jobless young men in work camps across the country. The monthly pay was $30. Each man received $5 for his personal expenses and $25 was deducted from his salary and sent directly to his family.

The CCC, which was designed primarily to help the unemployment problem, also carried out a broad conservation program throughout the United States. The young men repaired roads, built bridges, planted trees, built public parks and worked on a wide range of worthwhile projects to conserve the environment.

I recall Johnny Pechansky, our neighbor, all dressed up in khakis when he came home for a short leave from his CCC camp. He also brought along a friend who was in the CCC. The guys looked great to us kids and they also got some attention from the young ladies. (Raymond Burr and Walter Matthau were two young lads who worked in the CCC and later became famous.)

The lads in the CCC were all glad to have a job, even though they were temporary. They were now helping to support their families and they also had a little money to spend. The young men also felt more confident and optimistic about their lives.

Fred Baldino told me that his older brother Tony, Donald McCormick, and Billy Mader (all from Big Mine Run) served in the CCC.

The CCC was one of FDR's most popular New Deal programs. It was one that pleased the president, since he had a strong interest in conservation and felt the program would improve the national landscape. The CCC operated for 10 years and ended in 1942. During that time, it employed an average of 250,000 young men yearly, and over its lifetime approximately three million young men served in the program. The CCC helped many families, but it did not play a major role in decreasing unemployment. In *The Hungry Years,* T.H. Watkins wrote: "Only about 200,000 African Americans ever joined the CCC, representing about 7 percent of the total, substantially below the 10 percent goal that the CCC had established for black participation."

Wally Baran

Wally Baran and I grew up during the Depression. He was born and reared in Frackville, a small coal-mining town about six miles from Ashland. While I spent many summers living in Frackville with my Uncle Bill and Aunt Mary, I did not know him then. We each wrote a book, independently of one another, about growing up in the coal region.

Wally, now my friend, described his life in the CCC camp in his excellent book, *Feet First: A Memoir*. Wally had an older brother, Leonard, who served in the CCC. Wally also wanted to join, but was too young. However, by "fibbing" about his age (changing the date on his baptismal certificate) and manipulating his way through the physical examination, Wally managed to get into the CCC.

32. Wally Baran in the CCC, age 17.

Early in January 1941, he left the Pottsville Railroad Station, traveled to New Cumberland and then on to Virginia. From there he traveled across country to Montesano, Wash. It must have been an exciting trip for the youngest "coal cracker" on the train.

As it turned out, Wally had a successful career in the CCC. He was promoted to the rank of Leader, which was a responsible position for a lad of his age, and he earned $45 a month.

Wally went on to become a highly successful business magnate in the garment industry. Later he served in for eight years as Secretary of General Services for the Commonwealth of Pennsylvania in Governor Richard (Dick) Thornburgh's administration. Wally was also awarded two honorary doctorate degrees. I suspect that the $45 Wally earned each month in the CCC, which helped his mother get through those difficult times, gave him almost as much satisfaction as those large salaries he received as a garment tycoon.

33. Frackville lads in the CCC. Front row, from left: George Borzak, Jim Philips and Wally Baran. Back row, from left: Hal Roberts, Bill Evans, Ed "Bull" Papekia and Len Baran (Wally's brother).

Lynchings

The number of lynchings decreased drastically during a period of several decades leading up to the Depression. During the early and mid-Depression years, however, the practice briefly surged.

During the 1920s, there were 20 lynchings per year on average. The number of lynchings increased, reaching a maximum of 28 in 1933 and then declined afterward. Lynchings continued to decrease through the late 1940s and early 1950s, and were rare by the 1960s. Most of the lynchings occurred in the South, but a small number took place in the North.

34. Children in the Mississippi Delta Region, 1936.

The *Shenandoah Evening Herald*, Jan. 23, 1934:

NEGRO IS LYNCHED BY HAZARD, KY., MOB

Hazard, Ky., Jan. 23. (U.P) – Authorities today questioned six white men whose identities they concealed in connection with last night's "neck-tie party" in which Rex Scott, 20, negro, was executed for fatally wounding a white man.

Scott was lynched while his alleged victim, Alex Johnson, 32, still was fighting for his life in a local hospital. Johnson died of a fractured skull two hours after Scott's body was cut down.

The negro was strung up to a tree on the edge of a cemetery about 15 miles from here. The mob of 300 white men, some of whom were masked, took him from the local jail. While his body dangled, 28 shots were fired into it.

Scott was arrested Monday night after a street fight with Johnson. He allegedly struck Johnson over the head with a club when Johnson attempted to avenge a slurring remark Scott is said to have directed at Johnson's two women companions.

The *Shenandoah Evening Herald*, July 10, 1934:

LOUISIANA MOB HANGS NEGRO IN TOWN SQUARE

Bastrop, La., July 19. (U.P) – The body of a lynched negro was cut down from an oak tree in the public square today. Sheriff J. F. Carpenter said he recognized no member of the mob, which stormed parish Prison last night. District Attorney F. W. Hawthorne would not say what action he planned.

The negro, Andrew McCloud, 26, was suspected of an attempt to attack a white girl Saturday. The mob began forming at nightfall last night and within a few hours numbered 3,000. It tore down a telephone pole and used it to batter locks from doors.

The mob immediately went into action. While it was using the telephone pole as a ram, District Attorney Hawthorne arrived and made a speech.

"I sympathize with your attitude, but I'm afraid you'll get into trouble," he said.

"If you sympathize with us," one of the leaders shouted, "why don't you take off that straw hat and take a-hold of this telephone pole?"

Sheriff Carpenter and two deputies arrived and tried to dissuade the mob with no success.

Limp from a beating and blood gushing from a knife wound in the neck, McCloud was dragged out with a noose already around his neck. He was lifted to the top of an automobile, the free end of the rope tied to a limb, and the car driven from under him.

The *Shenandoah Evening Herald*, Oct. 27, 1934:

NEGRO LYNCHED AND MULITATED BY MOB OF 5,000

Lynching is Done in Swamp

Marianna, Fla., Oct. 27. (U.P.) – The body of Claude Neal, 23, negro, confessed attacker and slayer of a white girl, swung from a tree on the courthouse lawn here today, victim of lynch law.

A crowd of 100 men, women and children silently gazed at the body, nude except for a sack reaching from the waist to knees.

The negro had been shot at least 50 times, and burned with red-hot irons. The body had been dragged through the streets behind an automobile.

Later, a group of unidentified men appeared, cut down the mutilated body and removed it form the courthouse lawn.

Sheriff W. F. Chambliss, speaking from his home two blocks from the courthouse square, insisted he knew nothing of the lynching.

The *Shenandoah Evening Herald,* July 15, 1935:

TWO NEGROES LYNCHED IN MISSISSIPPI

Columbus, Miss., July 15. (U.P.) – A mob of white men, numbering fewer than 50, today lynched two negroes who purportedly confessed two attempts to attack a white woman near here.

The negroes, Ben Moore, 23, and Dooley Morton, 17, were taken from three deputies as they were being carried to Aberdeen, Miss. for safekeeping.

The mob in seven or eight automobiles quietly took the negroes back through Columbus toward Alabama before carrying them out a side road a short distance to hang them from a tree.

35. Cotton pickers in Arkansas.

The Early Mid-1930s

The Bast Colliery and "Bootlegging Coal"

The Bast Colliery in Big Mine Run had produced and shipped over 9.5 million tons of anthracite coal by 1928. During the 1920s, many collieries, owned by the large coal companies, were only working several days a week. So there was a recession in the Coal Region before the Great Depression began.

On May 15, 1934, there was an explosion at the Bast Colliery that killed one person and injured five others. The following day the Bast Mine was temporarily closed. There were plans, however, to open the mine at some future date.

In the meantime, plans got under way to extinguish a fire at the Bast that had been burning for many years. It turned out that they were unable to contain or put out the fire so that the miners could safely return to work. By the middle of August 1935, the Bast Mine was being abandoned for future operation.

Other collieries in the area were also facing hard times. Some were slowing down their operation or shutting down for short periods of time.

The *Shenandoah Evening Herald*, Aug. 27, 1935:

BAST MINE IS PREPARED FOR VIRTUAL ABANDONMENT

Work of preparing Bast mine of the Philadelphia and Reading Coal and Iron Company at Big Mine Run for virtual abandonment is now well under way.

Workmen are removing motors from the pumps and are taking down the big electric cable, which takes power into the mine down the slope. Miners whose tools were still inside the working [area] were notified this week to get them out.

These preparations are preliminary to flooding the mine from top to bottom in an effort to extinguish a fire, which has been burning for about 30 years.

Officials of the coal company a few weeks ago announced that recent flooding operations in a particular section of the mine had failed to extinguish the entire fire. They said at the time that they planned flooding the entire operation.

These operations will be very extensive and will require a great deal of time. Officials did not estimate just how long it will require for the mine to fill with water naturally.

36. The Bast Colliery in Big Mine Run.

    The economy, which had been bad, became further depressed. At the time, unemployment was at an all-time high and it was much higher in Big Mine Run and in the Coal Region in general. Unemployment in selected manufacturing industries was also higher.
    The unemployed coal miners began "bootlegging coal." Former miners started to mine coal without authorization on property owned by the coal companies. While bootlegging coal was illegal, it was quite common since the money earned from coal produced in this manner was the only means for unemployed miners to feed their families. These small bootlegging operations, which were generally carried out by just a few individuals (often by members of one family) were called "coal holes." Working in coal holes was very dangerous. In reading newspapers over a 10-year period during the Depression, it seemed there was a serious accident in a coal hole every week.

The *Shenandoah Evening Herald*, Aug. 3, 1934:

15-YEAR-OLD BOY IS KILLED IN COAL HOLE IN ATTEMPTING TO MAKE LIVING FOR FAMILY

The devotion of a 15-year-old youth to his widowed mother and his two younger brothers and a sister, in trying to keep the family larder filled, this morning shortly before the noon hour resulted in the tragic death of Joseph Yancius of Turkey Run, who as recently as March, last, persisted with his mother until he was permitted to leave the Freshman Class of the Shenandoah High School – that he might help the ones he loved.

The hand of fate fell heavily upon the Yancius family this morning about 11 o'clock, when the youth, who despite his tender years showed the sturdy qualities of a much older boy, was closed in at a make shift mine hole in a breach near Gilberton and about a half mile from the home where he was the main support.

There were many coal holes in Big Mine Run and the surrounding area. Some within a stone's throw of the miners' homes. William Michael Colahan, our neighbor, was seriously hurt in a coal hole only 100 yards from our home. I was 11 years old when we heard of his accident, which is described in the next two articles (everyone called him "Billy," however, the article referred to him by his middle name, Michael).

The Ashland Daily News, March 7, 1935:

2 Seriously Hurt In Accidents in Nearby Coal Holes

[William] Michael Colahan, 24, of Woodland Heights, near Big Mine Run, has a possible fracture of the back after being entombed for two hours in a hole yesterday afternoon.

Sylvester Kulkuskie, of Woodland Heights, yesterday afternoon was walking through the woods near Homesville. He noticed a mine hole, which had been closed by a fall of soft earth near the top.

Suddenly he heard a faint call for help. Attracted toward the hole he listened. The calls came more clearly from under the earth and Kulkuskie had no doubt that someone had been caught in the fall.

He went for aid at once and the work of opening the hole began. It was after three o'clock when [William] Michael Colahan was reached by rescue workers and removed to the Ashland State Hospital.

He had been trapped under the fall about 1 o'clock yesterday afternoon. Back injuries were the most serious the youth suffered and he was scheduled for x-ray examination at the hospital today to determine the extent of the injury.

The Ashland Daily News, May 21, 1935:

Woodland Heights Boy Dies at Hospital Here

[William] Michael, a son of Bridget and the late John Colahan, of Woodland Heights, died at the Ashland State Hospital last night following a short illness.

Surviving are his mother and five brothers: Thomas, of New York; John, of Locust Gap; Walter, of Shamokin; Edward, of Ashland; and Raymond, at home.

The *Shenandoah Evening Herald,* Sept. 13, 1939:

FATHER AND SON KILLED IN COAL HOLE ACCIDENT

Harvey Miller, 40, and his son, Tervine, 20, were killed instantly yesterday afternoon when covered by a fall of dirt at their coal hole near their home at Valley View.

Independent miners nearby recovered the bodies within a short time, but resuscitation efforts were futile. Robert Huntzinger, Valley View, one of the rescuers, suffered several fractured ribs when he slipped and fell.

The Millers were members of the United Brethren Church, Valley View.

Surviving the father are his widow, one daughter, three sons, his mother, one brother, and two sisters.

The *Shenandoah Evening Herald*, May 17, 1940:

2 MEN KILLED BY BLACK DAMP IN COAL HOLE

A bootleg miner and a fire boss who aided in attempts to rescue him lost their lives late yesterday afternoon in an improvised mine shaft on the mountainside southwest of Ashland. A third man narrowly escaped a similar fate.

Norman Umlauf, 27, Ashland, was overcome by black damp while descending the shaft and sustained a possible skull fracture when his limp body plunged to the bottom.

Andrew Wolfgang, 43, Lavelle, fire boss at Potts Colliery was also asphyxiated shortly after he had recovered Umlauf's body.

Earl Starr, of Ashland, a WPA employee who worked at the hole after his regular hours was overcome by the deadly fumes, but was revived and today was reported to be feeling no ill effects.

While waiting the arrival of Starr and Charles Kent who was also a WPA worker, Umlauf went down the shaft to fire a dynamite shot and then returned to the surface. By that time Starr had reached the top of the shaft and both men decided to prepare to load coal.

Umlauf had descended the shaft only about 15 feet when he was overcome and fell to the bottom. Starr, who saw Umlauf fall, immediately went to seek aid and met Kent walking toward the hole.

Attempting to make the rescue themselves, Kent tied a rope around Starr's body and started lowering him with the windlass used at the top of the shaft to hoist coal. Starr had only been down about 15 feet from the top when he was overcome, and Kent hoisted him to the surface and succeeded in reviving him.

Other bootleg miners were then summoned and a call was sent to the Potts Colliery for a rescue and first aid crew. The superintendent for the colliery responded by sending Arthur Dillman, a foreman, and Wolfgang, experienced in rescue work.

Using an oxygen mask to escape the gas, Wolfgang descended the shaft and fastened the rope around Umlauf's body. After the body was hoisted to the surface, rescue crews dropped the rope to Wolfgang, who tied it around himself and started the ascent.

Rescuers had pulled Wolfgang up to within 15 or 20 feet of the mouth of the shaft when they felt the rope becoming tight. Upon investigation, they discovered that he rope was tangled in a ladder and it required 10 minutes before it was possible to free Wolfgang. Finally, when they hoisted Wolfgang to the surface he was dead.

It is believed that the mask slipped off Wolfgang's face while he was being hoisted up the shaft.

Wolfgang is survived by his widow, Ethel, two sons and two daughters. Umlauf is survived by his widow, Carrie, a son and a daughter.

The *Shenandoah Evening Herald*, May 22, 1940:

ATLAS YOUTH KILLED IN BOOTLEG COAL HOLE

An Atlas youth lost his life late yesterday afternoon when he was crushed under a slide of frock in a bootleg coal hole located in a stripping between Byrnesville and Big Mine Run. It was his first day at work.

Charles Santelli, 21, was dead when rescuers reached him two hours later. His chest, body and legs were crushed.

A companion "Cotton" Washko, saw the slide and yelled, but Santelli was unable to escape and was covered.

Santelli is survived by his mother, one brother and three sisters.

The *Shenandoah Evening Herald*, July 31, 1934:

1,000 BOOTLEGGERS DEFY STATE POLICE

Pottsville, July 31 – At various points on the Good Spring Mountain this morning assembled an aggregation of between 1,000 and 1,800 coal bootleggers, who gathered to prevent coal and iron officers and State police officers from blasting shut holes in that section where bootlegging operations have been in progress for months past.

There were no holes blasted shut during the first several hours of the tryst, but officers were said to be preparing to blow the holes shut later in the day when the excitement subsided.

The members of the free mining fraternity gathered from all points south of the mountain and in several of the towns in the west end the scouts of the organization went along the streets ringing doorbells and giving the call to arms.

The State Police detail went west from the several sub-stations in eight cars and it was estimated that nearly 100 police were on the job.

The *Shenandoah Evening Herald*, Dec. 9, 1934:

BOOTLEG MINERS DYNAMITE SHAMOKIN STEAM SHOVEL

Shamokin, Pa. Dec. 5. (UP) – Operations of a strip coal mining company were at a standstill today following successful resistance of more than 2,000 miners who prevented the closing of "bootleg" coal holes on the Sevens Coal Company property.

A steam shovel, intended to be used in closing the shallow shafts, was dynamited and workmen from a Hazleton contracting firm were told to leave.

The blast, which wrecked the machine, did not injure the workmen.

The Stevens Company, operating the adjoining Cameron colliery, recently leased the land from the Lehigh Valley Coal Company and officials said it is necessary to close the coal holes, which honeycomb the property before starting underground operations.

Nearly 2,000 unemployed men have been working the land unmolested. A truck driver attempted to place a steam shovel on the ground for the coal company and was threatened. He returned to Shamokin and later was ordered back, in company with a state trooper.

He again was threatened and returned to the company headquarters. Then the shovel was blasted.

From time to time, however, the state police would take direct action against the bootleg miners and close the coal holes with dynamite.

The *Shenandoah Evening Herald,* July 16, 1934:

24 STATE POLICE HELP CLOSE BOOTLEG MINES

Coal company activities against bootleg mining were given added impetus today when, during the early morning hours, 24 State Police accompanied officers of the Lehigh Valley Coal Company into West Mahanoy Township and afforded protection to company employees while they "blew shut" 19 coal holes which were being operated in the Lost Creek stripping section.

It is reported that company police previously visited the scene, and when they were threatened by operators of the bootleg mines, called upon the State Police for protection.

So far as could be learned, blowing shut of the makeshift mining operations occurred only at Lost Creek, although reports were circulated that holes were to be closed in the Ellangowan section on Reading company properties.

The troopers were assigned here from the West Reading and Tamaqua barracks, and the training school at Hershey.

The *Shenandoah Evening Herald,* April 9, 1936:

BOOTLEG HOLES BLOWN SHUT AT GIRARDVILLE

Philadelphia and Reading Coal and Iron Company property guards used dynamite to blast shut several bootleg mines in and around Girardville Tuesday afternoon.

No disturbances of any kind were reported while the officers were blasting the independent workings.

The *Shenandoah Evening Herald*, Sept. 19, 1936:

28 BOOTLEG MINERS FREED BY GRAND JURY

Court House, Pottsville, Sept. 19. – Twenty-eight coal bootleggers were let go yesterday afternoon when the September Grand Jury ignored charges of unlawful mining of coal against them. Not only did the Grand Jury ignore the charges but also placed the costs of prosecution on the coal company policeman who brought the charges.

All the defendants are from Mahanoy City and vicinity and have been operating coal holes near that town on the property of the Lehigh Valley Coal Company. In an effort to break-up this practice the company arrested them on charges of violation of the mine laws. L. O. Spaid, a police officer of the coal company, was the prosecutor, and the Grand Jury, in ignoring the bills, directed that the costs be paid by him.

The *Shenandoah Evening Herald*, Feb. 17, 1937:

STATE POLICE ORDER BOOTLEG HOLES SHUT

Nine State Troopers from the Tamaqua and Reading barracks stopped two large bootleg operations near the highway at Maizeville today, ordering the mouths dynamited and filled with dirt.

No arrests were made or contemplated, the troopers said. More than 20 men were employed at the operations, which had existed for almost four years. It was estimated that 20 tons were produced daily from each of the makeshift mines located on Maderia Hill Company grounds north of the bottom of the Maizeville hill.

The troopers reported one tunnel extended 280 feet, endangering the highway, railroad and a residence. Also that Maizeville residents had complained bitterly of the dynamite blasts which they feared.

The men were warned on several occasions, stated the state police, and ignored the orders each time.

The *Shenandoah Evening Herald,* Aug. 14, 1937:

COAL COMPANY POLICE BLAST 18 HOLES SHUT

Coal company police, accompanied by State Motor Police, blasted eighteen "bootleg" coal holes shut near Tremont yesterday. No violence was threatened by independent miners as they watched the dynamiting.

The holes shut were in barrier pillars or coal reserves, which are left standing in compliance with state laws to prevent the spread of fire or floods from one mine to another. It was for this reason that Mine Inspector James Grace of Heckschersville ordered the holes blasted.

After grade school let out, I would go looking for small pieces of coal that might be scattered around at the coal holes on the hill behind our home. When my 100-pound burlap bag was full, I would haul it home in my homemade wheelbarrow. I would go around the neighborhood and sell my coal for twenty-five cents a bag. Many years later my respectable salary as a college professor did not give me more satisfaction than those twenty-five cent sales I made back then, when I was 10- or 11-years-old.

Anthracite Coal Breakers

The entire anthracite region was dotted with coal breakers. A typical breaker was a tier-shaped structure, which had black siding and roofing, and windows that are always covered with coal dust. The coal breaker was the largest building on the colliery premises; there, the coal was crushed, cleaned and prepared for shipment. There were other smaller breakers throughout the region that were not part of a colliery that also processed coal (including bootleg coal) for shipment.

37. The St. Nicholas Breaker.

The St. Nicholas Breaker, located midway between Shenandoah and Mahanoy City on route 45, was unusual since the siding was light gray. It was the largest coal beaker in the world when it went into operation in 1932 at a cost of $5 million. It produced 12,500 tons of coal daily and operated for 31 years until it closed in 1964.

Christmas Time

Our family as well as other Ukrainian families celebrated Christmas on Jan. 7, which followed the old Julian calendar. It was a holiday steeped in religious tradition and celebrated with various customs. On Dec. 25, we greeted each other by saying, "Merry Christmas." On Jan. 7, when we entered another Ukrainian household, we said, "Chrystos rodyvsya" or "Christ is born." The person greeting the visitor would the say, "Slavite Yoho" or Let us glorify Him. Kids often made fun of us for celebrating Christmas two weeks after they did.

My mother prepared a huge meal on Christmas Eve with 12 separate non-meat food dishes, all of which had religious significance. It was one of those special religious holidays when we ate very well. Mom also made a popular alcoholic drink called "boilo." The ingredients included orange and lemon juice, honey, cloves and lots of whiskey. It was the mother of all hot toddy drinks.

Sometime during the holiday season, a small group of singers visited each Ukrainian home and sang Christmas carols in Ukrainian. Our family also joined in with the singers.

Despite family tradition, our parents allowed us to celebrate Christmas on Dec. 25, and any presents we got were always placed under the Christmas tree on that date. If I received a store-bought present, it was usually a shirt or sweater – something useful. I did, however, always get some fruit, nuts and candy along with a few lumps of coal in my stocking, which back then was not considered a bad thing. Even though I was quite young I didn't expect much. Christmas was a happy time.

During the 1930s we always had a large Sears and Roebuck mail order catalog at home. It was the size of a fairly large phone directory and contained hundreds and hundreds of items. I was fond of looking through it and saying, "I would like to have this and I would like to have that."

About a month before Christmas I would look through the catalog almost daily. I saw toys, a cowboy uniform, and other things I wanted. My family was not able to purchase items like that and frankly that did not bother me. It was, however, fun just to look through that catalog and do some wishful dreaming.

38. Christmas dinner at the Earl Pauley home in Smithland, Iowa, 1935.

One Christmas Eve we went to bed, however, we did not put up a decorated Christmas tree as we usually did. About 11:30 that night my father came home with a Christmas tree (he had a few drinks before he arrived). Mom quickly woke us up and told us to bring all the Christmas decorations from the attic. After we finished decorating our tree sometime in the wee hours on Christmas Day, we went to bed. When I woke up on Christmas Morning, I felt that Santa had indeed stopped by.

The *Shenandoah Evening Herald*, Dec. 23, 1938:

Jobless Father Loses Life Trying To Get Xmas Tree

Grafton, Ohio, Dec. 23. (U.P.) – An 84-year-old farmer today shot to death an unemployed father and wounded the man's wife, authorities said, as the couple attempted to take a Christmas tree from his farm for their children. The farmer then fled.

The victims were Carl Rousseau, 37, and his wife, Minnie, 29, parents of girls, ages 11 and 8.

Sheriff Carl Finnegan, of Lorain County, said the couple fell from a shotgun blast fired by Will Case.

Finnegan said Case had walked to the home of his nearest neighbor, Leland Martin, and said, "I just shot a couple of guys trying to steal some more of my trees. Call the constable and tell him they are lying on the road."

Constable Lyman Hitchcock, of Columbia Township, was first to arrive. He said Rousseau was slumped dead over the front wheel of the couple's old automobile by the roadside. Mrs. Rousseau, he said, was leaning against the car moaning.

"I'm shot," she told him, "get some help."

Hitchcock said he had called Sheriff Finnegan before going out, but that by the time he had assisted Mrs. Rousseau, and the sheriff had arrived, neither could find Case. Deputies then began a search.

The shooting occurred at 2:45 a.m. when the couple was returning home after spending the evening with relatives in Cleveland. The relatives told Finnegan that the couple had managed to save a few coins to buy Ten-Cent-Store gifts for their children, Geraldine and Rose.

Finnegan said the presents were stacked neatly in the back seat when he discovered the tragedy. By their side was an inexpensive string of lights to go on a Christmas tree.

"The Case place has a lot of pine trees," the sheriff said. "As they passed there they decided apparently to cut down one so their kids would have a tree for Christmas."

The tree laid in the ditch by the roadside and by it a saw Rousseau had used.

"Apparently, they were walking back to their car when the old man saw them." Finnegan said. "He must have been lying in wait to guard his trees, because only two shots were fired."

One hit Rousseau in the back and the other his wife in the right side.

Mrs. Rousseau was semi-conscious when taken to a hospital in nearby Elyria. On the way she said: "I know we should have bought the tree for the children, but we've been so hard up. There are a few presents in the back of the car. Please see that the children get them if I die."

Easter

We also celebrated Easter on two different dates. Whenever a Ukrainian family visited us on Easter, they would say, "Chrystos voskres" or "Christ has risen." Then we would say, "Voistinu Voskres" or "Indeed He is risen."

Mom did a lot of special cooking and baking for the Easter holidays. I can still remember the wonderful smell of freshly baked bread as Mom lifted the loaves out of the oven. One special loaf, called paska was about one foot high and one foot in diameter. Each family took their own paska to the church to be blessed.

At Easter I got a basket with some of our own colored eggs, a few homemade coconut Easter eggs, some jelly beans and a small store-bought chocolate Easter bunny.

Of course we colored eggs with dye. We began with about six ordinary drinking glasses and then added warm water to each until they were all about two-thirds full. Then we placed a small dye pill into each glass. After the pill dissolved, we would place an egg into the water, wait for a while, and remove it. We would compete to see who could make the best-looking egg.

Then we would crack each other's egg for fun. The person who ended up with the cracked egg was the loser. I had a purple wooden egg and my buddy, Nicky Pechansky, had a solid glass eggs. When we attempted to crack each other's eggs – nothing happened. It was a standoff and we would laugh. Life was much simpler then.

Mom

My Mother had a difficult life growing up in Poland. Her family lived in poverty and she never went to school, so she could not read or write. When she came to America in 1912 she still had a difficult time because she was alone and illiterate. Those difficult times evidently helped her and many, many others who had similar experiences to get through the Depression in America.

My Mom was very industrious and resourceful. She somehow kept our family together; she managed our household very well considering how little she had. I feel that she, like many women had a very difficult time making ends meet. On top of their duties at home, many mothers also had to work outside the home (usually house cleaning) to earn money because their unemployed husbands simply could not find work.

Mom did housecleaning in three different households to help out financially. She worked for Frank Burke (mortician), John Shovlin (principal of Kulpmont High

School) and the Anna and Leo Almond family, all residents of Ashland. Practically all of my memories of Mom are thoughts and images of her working. It seems she worked all the time – but then, she had no choice. Sometimes she would take me with her when she went housecleaning. I soon learned that I wasn't there to watch, but to dust, and dust some more.

We also did the laundry for those three households. She believed that her four children should do our share of the work. There were no automatic washers or dryers. Our washing machine, which ran on electricity, had a wringer attached to it. The wringer consisted of two powered hard rubber rollers that pressed very tightly together. Even as a youngster I very carefully fed the wet clothes through the wringer before hanging them on the clothesline in our back yard. Mom always reminded me to be careful not to allow my fingers to get caught in the fast moving rollers.

When we hung the clothes, we always folded them over a little and then fastened them on the line with a clothespin. In the winter I would help take the frozen clothes off of the clothesline. I actually had to pry off the frozen clothing with my fingers. It was stiff and difficult to handle. You could not fold the frozen sheets outside; you had to take them inside the house and let them soften.

On washing days our home had three ironing boards in use at the same time. We only had one electric iron; the others we heated on our coal stove (everything that was washed was also ironed in those days). As a youngster, I was allowed to iron simple pieces like handkerchiefs, dish towels and other flat pieces; not shirts or things like that.

One day when I was quite young, I noticed my Mom touching the moistened palm of her hand against the hot iron. I heard a slight hissing sound and I thought she had burned herself. She told me that she was only testing the iron to see if it was hot enough to start ironing the clothes. When I understood what she was doing, I felt better but somehow it always bothered me when I saw her do that.

Making Soap

Since Mom did the laundry for three households, it was much cheaper to use homemade soap for washing clothes. She taught me how to make soap; my three sisters didn't get involved in this chore. Her ability to make soap was only one of many things she did; my father rarely helped in doing anything like that.

To create soap, she collected fats from meat and other fatty substances, which she heated on our coal stove. After it liquefied and cooled somewhat (but was still warm) I was allowed to pour the contents into a large circular porcelain bowl. Then I slowly poured lye from a can into the liquefied fat and constantly stirred the contents with a large wooden spoon. During the mixing, the dark brown liquefied fat turned a creamy color and thickened. After that, I set the bowl aside and let it solidify.

After a few days, I used a large flat blade knife to loosen the edge of the 30-pound cake of soap from the inside of the bowl, and then cut the soap into bars.

I always felt satisfied when I completed a task like that or any of the other many things Mom taught me to do. She taught me well, not only to start something, but also to finish it.

Quitting School

Many children had to leave school to help support their families. There was no other choice. My oldest sister, Hattie, had to quit attending Ashland High School in the mid-1930s because she had to support our family. It was sad because she was a good student and talented in mathematics. Hattie cried when she had to leave school because she enjoyed learning and was doing so well, and that's the way it was. Getting a job to help one's family took precedence over education.

Hattie's first job was as a housekeeper. She was paid $3 a week. Later, she worked at a factory (located at the bottom of town) in Ashland, which made men's shirts and pajamas.

If she had the opportunity to complete high school she would have been an excellent college student, but there was no money for higher education.

As she grew older and we got around to talking about the past, she always regretted that she was not able to finish high school. Then, with a little smile, she would mention that she cold always add up a column of numbers (in her head, no calculator) faster than anyone else could.

Not too long after that, my second-oldest sister, Mary, also stopped attending public school, for the same reason. Fortunately, my youngest sister Anna and I had the opportunity to graduate from high school and we both have our older sisters to thank for that.

39. A school in Alabama, 1935.

Many of the youngsters I attended grade school with went on to high school for a year or two and the quit. Kids often skipped class, and some of my classmates took off all holidays, regardless of the religious denomination. Sometimes after a practice fire drill, some guys didn't return to class.

The *Shenandoah Evening Herald*, Dec. 23, 1937:

PUPILS' EXIT IS QUICK RETURN IS SLOW... AHEM

A surprise fire drill at the J. W. Cooper High School yesterday afternoon brought out every pupil to the street in one minute and 20 seconds – a record time or thereabouts which was highly commended by Supt. A. J. Ratchford, who used a stop-watch to time the exodus.

But – it required two minutes and 40 seconds, or twice as long, for the boys and girls to get back. Why? Fine weather and the Christmas spirit, seriously thought Mr. Ratchford. The boys and girls had an answer, too. Doesn't the way back always seem longer?

In accordance with the state law, Principal Bernard Leach said, at least one fire drill will be held every month. Each will come as a surprise. So the school authorities think. But the pupils tell each other: "Be ready anytime for that gong when the weather is nice."

The Economy Still Depressed

40. Long lines of unemployed workers were common.

The *Shenandoah Evening Herald*, Oct. 19, 1934:

26,853 UNEMPLOYED IN COUNTY, RELIEF SURVEY DISCLOSES

Of 83,394 employable persons enumerated during April, 1934, in Schuylkill County, 32.2 per cent, or 26,853, were unemployed seeking work; 50.2 per cent. or 41,822 were employed full time, and 17.6 per cent, or 14,719, were employed part time.

Shenandoah Borough had more unemployed than any other community in Schuylkill County in April of this year, according to a survey, made by the State Emergency Relief Board. There were 3,573 out of work in this borough at the time of the survey, or 43.7 percent of the employable population of the town.

41. Men hanging out in a shack in N.Y. Note the small Christmas tree.

The *Shenandoah Evening Herald*, Sept. 3, 1934:

23,000,000 TO NEED RELIEF THIS WINTER

By Lyle C. Wilson
United Press Correspondent

Washington, Sept. 3. (U.P.) – President Roosevelt is confronted today by an appalling human relief crisis revealed in a new deal report that 23,000,000 persons–men, women and children–will need aid to live through next winter.

Resort to some extraordinary emergency relief method similar to last winter's [Civil Works Administration] appears inevitable. It probably will be started in November.

Donald L. Richberg, secretary of the Executive Council, cited the unprecedented problem in a report to Mr. Roosevelt on relief of destitution since January 1, 1933. Richberg said: "Federal, state and local relief costs for 1933 and the first six months of 1934 were $1,338,665,566. [Further] 5,000,000 families are expected on the relief rolls by February 1935.

42. Men eating in a soup kitchen in Washington, D.C.

The *Shenandoah Evening Herald*, Nov. 5, 1934:

NEW DEAL SPENDING NEARS 11 BILLION

By Richard L. Gridley
United Press Staff Correspondent

Washington, Nov. 5. (U.P.) – Federal expenditures under the new deal neared $11,000,000,000 today as recovery costs were shown to have already run the government "in the red" to the extent of $5.600,000,000.

Thus, in the first 20 months of the new deal, the administration has piled up the largest deficit in peacetime history. It is prepared to spend at least $6,000,000,000 more in its effort to lick the depression.

43. A line-up for soup and bread.

After six years of economic depression, our family was still struggling. My father, who was unemployed for some time, now had miners' asthma and it was difficult for him to get even part-time work. The income from housecleaning work done by my mother and sisters, which wasn't that great, was all we had. The uncertainty of it all – not knowing what lies ahead – was worse than the truth.

I was about 11 years old and in the sixth grade. I was now beginning to understand more clearly not only that we were poor, but that many others also were having a difficult time getting along. Furthermore, I began to read and hear more things about the Depression and realized that it was a nation-wide problem.

Sometimes a poor, shabbily dressed man (never a woman) came around looking for something to eat. He was simply a poor guy who was non-threatening and wanted a handout. He would take anything. Even though we were poor ourselves, Mom would find something to give him. She realized that he had less than we had.

The Ashland Daily News, Jan. 22, 1935:

Clothing Needed in Which to Bury Locust Dale Girl

Unless friends come to the family's rescue immediately 8-year-old Lillian Andressky, near Locust Dale, will be buried in very poor funeral raiment.

The child died yesterday in the Ashland State Hospital and arrangements for the funeral have been completed.

With 11 other children in the family, Mrs. Mary Andressky has been found in dire need. An appeal has been made for aid to the local Red Cross but in fear that this appeal can not be acted upon in time for the funeral tomorrow any person who can make donations of clothing, food, or money is asked to do so at the store of Charles Boppel at 261 Centre Street in Ashland.

Not only is clothing needed for the dead girl's shroud but for other children in the family as well.

Three articles from the *Shenandoah Evening Herald* in 1934:

COUNTERFEIT 50-CENT PIECES ARE REPORTED

The circulation of counterfeit 50-cent pieces, reported at Tamaqua, resulted in a police teletype warning being sent out to merchants throughout the region to be on the alert for the spurious coins.

It is a poor imitation of the genuine coin, being dark, heavy, and smooth, and is easily detected if the least bit of care is taken.

NEW COUNTERFEIT $5 BILL CIRCULATED IN THIS AREA

Local banks have received notice from the United Sates Treasury Department of a new counterfeit five-dollar bill discovered in circulation. [It was] termed a good likeness of real money.

COUNTERFEIT $10 BILLS ARE BEING CIRCULATED

Counterfeit $10 bills have made their appearance in the lower anthracite region and all merchants and others are cautioned to beware when accepting notes of this denomination.

The counterfeits are fairly good imitations and are not easily detected, especially when accepted in haste by a business merchant.

When compared with a good $10 note, however, the fraud becomes apparent. The paper of the counterfeit money does not bear the colored silk threads of a good note, the ink is lighter, and the face of Hamilton is smudgy.

The *Shenandoah Evening Herald*, Sept. 28, 1936:

FRACKVILLE MEN HELD FOR COUNTERFEITNG

Charged with making and circulating counterfeit five-cent coins of lead, three Frackville and two Morea men were sent to county prison awaiting a hearing before United States Commissioner Reese at Tamaqua.

The men are: David Bowen Jr. Joseph Yesalusky and Albert Chevinsky, Frackville and William Derricott and William Kerrigan of Morea.

They were arrested Saturday by U. E. Baughman of the United States Secret Service, assisted by Sergeant J. C. Grey and Corporals Arthur Ditchfield and R. A. Walters of the State Highway Patrol.

Bowen and Kerrigan are accused of manufacturing the illicit coins, while Chevinsky and Yesalusky are charged with passing them. Derricott, a taxidermist, was named as the one who made the molds in which the spurious coins were cast.

Now, 70-some years later, we're in the midst of a recession. When I go to Burger King in Shippensburg for coffee I see a small sign, posted for customers to see. I mentioned to Patty Flemistr, the manager that I wanted to use the sign in my book. She graciously gave me a copy. It reads:

DUE TO A NUMBER OF COUNTERFEIT BILLS, WE WILL NOT ACCEPT HUNDRED DOLLAR BILLS

It's a small but clear-cut example of what it was like then – and now.

44. A family on the move with no destination.

Works Progress Administration (WPA)

45. Women workers in a WPA sewing project.

By the mid-1930s, direct aid in the form of relief was not solving the country's economic problems. Since unemployment was still high, FDR decided to promote work relief. In 1935 he changed the government's relief policy. Instead of providing direct relief, the government provided work relief by way of the Works Progress Administration (WPA). FDR felt it was better for a person's dignity to have a job and a sense of purpose rather than just receiving a handout. He announced his work relief program in one of his fireside chats.

Burton W. Folsom wrote, "[The] WPA cost taxpayers over $4.8 billion in the 1935 appropriation (almost 15 percent of the entire national debt)."

The WPA was a massive public works project to help promote an economic recovery. The men built roads, bridges, dams, schools, airports, landing strips and other infrastructure. The WPA also operated a Federal Art Project, which employed actors, musicians, writers and artists.

Many women who headed families and needed help desperately (often a forgotten group) were also employed. Women worked in factories, medical facilities, schools and libraries, including traveling librarians. Author T. H. Watkins pointed out that the WPA set up thousands of sewing centers all over the country. By February 1936, 294,532 women were employed making clothing, sheets blankets, pillows and other similar items.

The *Shenandoah Evening Herald*, Sept. 15, 1936:

BUTLER TWP. AWARDED $32,727 GRANT BY PWA

G. Douglas Andrews, state WPA [Works Progress Administration] director, announced that today the Washington office of the Public Works Administration authorized the payment of $32,727.25 to the School District of Butler Township in Schuylkill County.

Although $103,909 will be expended in the construction of this modern high school building, the people of Butler Township will be required to pay only $72,000, since the Public Works Administration is contributing $58,909 or 45 percent of the total cost of the project.

The benefits to Butler Township and Ashland are numerous. These needed school facilities are being provided at a great saving to the local taxpayers. At the same time, approximately 81,000 man-hours of useful site employment have been created, an amount sufficient to employ over 70 men for a whole year. In addition, local shopkeepers are benefiting through the increased purchasing power of the employed workers.

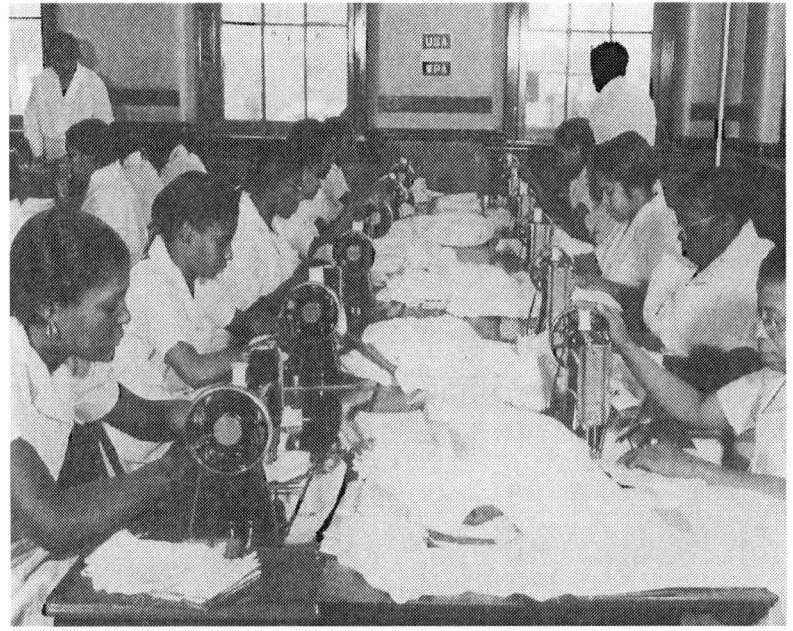

46. Women employed by the WPA in Louisville, Kentucky.

The new Butler Township High School was located just off route 61 about halfway between Ashland and Fountain Springs. I was in the second graduating class in June 1942.

The *Shenandoah Evening Herald*, Oct. 17, 1935:

LOCAL WOMEN TO GET WORK ON WPA ROLLS

Sewing projects that will supply work for 130 local women now on relief rolls are being pressed for approval by the Shenandoah Board of Education, Superintendent A. J. Ratchford announced today, along with word of seven other school projects that are being worked out.

Fifty women will be given work in one of the sewing projects, using material that may be contributed locally. Eighty more would work on materials to be furnished by the national Works Progress Administration womens' division.

The big difficulty facing school officials now is to find room to begin the projects. There would be no home sewing in these projects.

Clothing that can be supplied to families on relief rolls will be the principal output of the project. The women will be paid a monthly wage of $55.

Wally Baran told me this story about his mother, Antoinette. She was one of about 25 other ladies who were employed by the WPA. The women operated sewing machines in a basement room that had been a "company store" owned and operated by one of the large coal companies. The women did their sewing on their own foot-operated sewing machines, which they brought from home. I'm sure that those monthly wages were not only well earned, but also highly appreciated.

47. WPA workers made mattresses from Spanish moss in Savannah, Ga.

I was not aware of anyone from Big Mine Run that was employed by the WPA. Wanda Kehler Edelman, my classmate at Butler Township High School, reminded me that musicians employed by the WPA performed several concerts at our high school when we were students there. Lee Berger, who was from Schuylkill Haven, led the orchestra.

There was no major WPA project going on in Big Mine Run. That was most likely true of many other patch towns. In Ashland, however, there is a beautiful, one-of-a-kind Mothers' Memorial. The WPA built the distinctive stone structure and steps that lead up to the impressive bronze statue from street level. I often walked from Big Mine Run to Ashland and walked up the steps, around the Mothers' Memorial, and back down to the street (a partial but impressive list by state of some highlights of the WPA can be found in the book *American-Made* by Nick Taylor).

48. Stone construction and steps built by the WPA in Ashland, Pa.

In 1935, the WPA began building the Catocin Recreational Demonstration Area project near Thurmont, Md; it became known as Hi-Catocin. During World War II, FDR picked Hi-Catocin as a retreat to get away from the Washington, D.C. for short periods. FDR renamed the camp Shangri-La in 1942 after some additional improvements had been made.

In 1953, President Eisenhower changed the name to Camp David in honor of his grandson. Little did the WPA workers realize that the campsite they worked on would serve as a retreat for some of the most important leaders of the world, a tradition that continues to this day.

49. FDR and Winston Churchill at Shangri-la on May 14, 1943.

During its lifetime, the WPA accomplished a great deal. It created many socially useful projects, and its rich legacy can still be seen in many places throughout the country.

The WPA, however, was the most criticized of the New Deal programs. The workers were mocked and referred to as "boondogglers," accused of doing pointless and unnecessary work. Critics were often heard to say that WPA stood for "We Piddle Around."

In June 30, 1943, it was all over and the WPA simply went away – not with a bang, but a with a whimper. The following brief on page nine of *The New York Times* did not do justice to the program.

The New York Times, July 1, 1943:

WPA PAYS UP AND QUITS

Washington, June 30 AP – The Work Projects Administration turned back $130,000,000 to the Treasury today and went out of existence.

Only a small "liquidation staff" of the relief agency remained at the end, getting records and accounts into shape for a final report on its operations.

The records will show, officials said, that WPA spent about $10,500,000,000 and employed 8,500,000 persons since its inception in 1935.

The refund to the Treasury, they said, was $105,000,000 in unexpended funds and $25,000,000 in supplies and material.

Social Security

Several months after Roosevelt started the WPA program, he signed the bill creating the Social Security System. It was an insurance plan (a social safety net) for the unemployed, aged and disabled based on both employee and employer contributions. Prior to social security, most Americans faced a future of economic hardship and uncertainty. FDR's social security plan was a major step toward guaranteeing people some economic security. He was the first president to advocate protection for the elderly.

When I learned about social security as a youngster, I didn't seriously think about it since it was something too far in the future. I never thought I would collect any financial benefits from the system. In my retirement years, as is the case now, I am indeed receiving social security benefits.

Initially, social security was designed to focus on unemployment, but it was controversial because some felt it would result in a loss of jobs. It has evolved primarily as a means of support for retirees and the disabled.

Unemployment compensation benefits began in the spring of 1936, but benefits for retirees did not begin until January 1940. Social Security is FDR's most famous piece of legislation and it has become the most popular social program in American history.

Some estimates predict that revenue from workers and employers going into the Social Security trust fund will continue to exceed benefits for only two more decades or until the year 2037. After that, social security will be making the federal budget deficit larger. This problem has been discussed frequently; it's a serious problem and needs to be addressed sometime soon. Employees presently contributing to social security need to be covered when they reach retirement age.

Women Step Up

FDR appointed Frances Perkins as Secretary of Labor shortly after he was inaugurated. She had just walked into history; the first woman to serve in the president's Cabinet. Perkins (who did not have the right to vote until she was 40-years-old) served for 12 years; she left one month after FDR's death in 1945.

The *Shenandoah Evening Herald*, Aug. 22, 1930:

TWO GIRLS APPEARED TODAY WEARING SHORTS

Some of the old fashioned communities in the country have put a ban on "shorts" for girls, but in most communities they have been approved for warm weather by the fair sex.

Today two local lassies stepped forth with "shorts" and for a while it looked like a traffic jam would occur, but as the girls walked about the streets they soon were left to their own comfort, or could it be called discomfort.

This is the second time that a representative of the Herald has seen "shorts" being worn by women in Shenandoah this summer. Last week two young women came bravely down the [Shenandoah] Heights road while everyone, especially the males, seemed to enjoy the change in summer wear for women.

The Ashland Daily News, June 7, 1933:

Penniless Mother
Found Wheeling 2
Babies 270 Miles
Distant From Home

Providence, R. I. (UP) — With a road map to guide her and a solitary sandwich to sustain her, a

Philadelphia mother, wheeling two babies in a perambulator toward her home 270 miles away, was halted by a policeman here today.

At police headquarters, Mrs. Barbra Rostovich, 36, Philadelphia, told the story:

One of her two babies, 21-months-old and 7 months-old, respectively, had required medical treatment obtainable only in Boston. She and her husband had pooled their resources and she had gone to Boston and obtained the treatment.

Last night she bought a bus ticket form Boston to Providence, had the driver put her baby carriage on the bus roof, and came here. She then spent her last dime for a sandwich, obtained a free road map, and began the long homeward hike.

Reaching Roger Williams Park, she inquired of motorcycle officer Walter J. Manning whether she was on Route 1. When he learned her destination he took her and her babies to headquarters.

The Rostovich family was put to bed in a hotel. Later today the mother was to be given a ticket to Philadelphia by a loving relief agency.

50. Oklahoma mother with her child.

The Ashland Daily News, July 7, 1933:

Woman, 55, Walks 6 Miles
To Earn $2.25 Per Week

By PAUL COMLY FRENCH

Philadelphia, (U.P.) – With labor protesting sweatshop conditions in the mills of eastern Pennsylvania, the joint legislative committee investigating starvation wages and long hours throughout the state reconvened at Norristown for a public meeting. Yesterday the committee held a hearing at Doylestown. At the same time a special state commission studying the administration of the workmen's compensation act opened its second day of hearings in Philadelphia.

The highlight of the testimony before the sweatshop investigating committee came when Mrs. Geo. Scholl, 55, a coat finisher, explained how she worked two hours daily without punching the time clock.

"I get in at 6 A. M.," she testified, "and work until seven before I ring in on the clock. Then at night I work one hour after I punch the clock."

Her average wage, she said, was $2.25 weekly.

"I have earned as high as $3.30," she added.

The 55-year-old woman, who walks six miles to work from Sellersville to a Quakertown factory, said she had to water several hundred turkeys before going to work.

"I get my board for watering the turkeys" she explained in answer to a question of Mrs. Gifford Pinchot, wife of the Governor and a member of the commission.

In the Waxman Shirt Company's factory, Quakertown, the commission was told, girls and boys working as trimmers average $3 to $4 a week.

"Eighty girls work in the plant," a witness said, "and 50 percent of them average less than $5 weekly."

In the Perkiomen Leather Company, Quakertown, boys earn 8 cents an hour making pocketbooks while wages in the Trum-Sellersville Dress Company, near Quakertown, average from $3.50 to $6.00 a week

The *Shenandoah Evening Herald*, Jan. 26, 1934:

ELOPE AT 3 P.M., PART AT 7:05; WIFE GETS DIVORCE

Camden, N. J., Jan. 26. (U.P.) – Zola Bryen, 20, succeeded in having her marriage to Murray Bidner, 24, annulled when she described the following time-table of events:

At 3:00 p. m. they eloped.
At 4:00 p. m. she went to a movie alone
At 6:30 p. m. they dined together.

At 7:00 p. m. he confessed that he lied about his wealth.

At 7:05 p. m. she went back to mother.

The Ashland Daily News, Feb. 1, 1934:

Forced to Quit As Coal Miner

Ohio's only woman coal miner, Ida Mae Stull, 34, who has been banished from her job in the Cadiz, Ohio, mine, shown below her photo, because state law forbids women working in mines, and has been "sentenced" to housework, which she detests. A miner since she was 12, Miss Stull has loaded five tons of coal daily.

(Her independent spirit led her to take action in court to get back her job of mining n the hills of Ohio. She made a special appeal to Governor George White. Attorney General, John Bricker, ruled that she was allowed to continue mining coal because she was the owner of the mine.)

51. The woman coal miner.

The *Shenandoah Evening Herald*, Aug. 17, 1936:

Woman 75, Walks Two Miles To Get Injury Sewed Up

Worcester, Mass., Aug. 17. (U.P.) – Her left hand mangled by the wringer of a washing machine, Mrs. Joseph Archambault, 75, walked two miles to police headquarters today, refused an anesthetic, and sat without a murmur while a police surgeon took 13 stitches in the hand.

"That didn't hurt a bit," she said as she spurned a ride home. "People today don't know [what] pain is."

The *Shenandoah Evening Herald*, Feb. 24, 1936:

Working Girl Can Dress Herself on $1.50 Weekly

New York, Feb. 24. (U.P.) – The Association for Improving the Condition of the Poor, which announced a few months ago that a working girl could eat all she needed for $2.25 a week, asserted today that she can dress for $1.50 a week.

The association specified in detail the coats, suits, nightgowns and other textile items a girl needs "for health and decency," but skipped such items as rouge and lipstick.

The working girl budget was computed with the assumption that a $12.50 winter coat would last two years and a $5 spring coat three years. The girl was supposed to make 15 pair of silk stockings last a year, but the association thought she needed four pairs of shoes, four dresses and three hats.

All the ends of "health and decency" would be served with 10-cent garters and $1 girdles, the association said, effecting considerable savings from the sums girls frequently allowed themselves for such items.

The association's complete wardrobe for the working girl was:

Three hats at $2; one winter coat $12.50; one spring coat, $5; four dresses, $5 each; two smocks at 90 cents; four vests at 25 cents; four pair of bloomers or step-ins at 35 cents; two nightgowns at 60 cents; two girdles or corsets at $1; four pair of shoes at $3 ($4.20 additional allowed for repairs); one pair rubbers, $1; one pair bedroom slippers, 90 cents; 15 pair silk stockings at 80 cents; two pair of garters at 10 cents; 12 handkerchiefs at 5 cents; two pair gloves at 85 cents; two pocketbooks at $1; one umbrella, $1.

The rubbers and bedroom slippers were expected to last two years, the umbrella three years.

The *Shenandoah Evening Herald,* Aug. 7, 1937:

Girl Swims Four Miles in Rough Seas To Save 3

New York, Aug. 7. (U.P.) – A 19-year-old girl swam four miles through heavy seas early today to summon aid for her sweetheart and two friends who had been thrown into the ocean when their motor launch capsized.

Coast Guardsmen and lifesavers rescued her companions off Far Rockaway Beach shortly before dawn.

The girl, Marjorie Murray of Woodmere, N.Y., was near exhaustion when she reached the beach and reported the accident to Albert Allspach, who had been fishing in the surf.

Miss Murray and her fiancée, Arnold McCloat, 21, had accompanied Helen McNiff, 19, and John Jancoski, 22, on a moonlight cruise in Jancoski's launch, Mary Ann. They were not aware of Coast Guard warnings that the sea was too rough for small boats.

The boat developed motor trouble, Miss Murray said, and finally the engine stopped. It was tossed about by the waves. Water rolled over it, and was filling the cabin. The men told the girls to put on life preservers.

An expert swimmer, she tread water until a wave tossed her high enough so that she could see the lights on the Rockaway boardwalk. She kicked off her beach pajamas and shoes and struck out for shore.

Allspach summoned coastguards-men, who sent 10 boats through the breakers to aid Miss Murray's companions. McCloat was found clinging to the overturned boat.

"It was like a match box out at sea," he said.

All were taken to a coast guard station, then to a hospital to be treated for fatigue and exposure.

The high unemployment figures throughout the Depression were a serious problem. The unemployed men felt discouraged because there were very few prospects for a job. The men felt helpless and worthless because they couldn't provide for their families. Some men would leave home and look for work all day, only to return empty handed to face their hungry children. And there were many times when these idle men would just gather together and talk about the uncertainty of their future.

On the other hand, most women were constantly busy doing all the household chores and trying to feed their families on what little they had. They stretched everything to make ends meet. The ends didn't always meet, because you can only stretch things so far. But mothers, being mothers, somehow managed. They did without many things, but having babies (in many cases) was not one of them.

Many women also stepped up and played a key role in earning income by doing work outside their homes. So a "woman's work" was no longer only what she did in her own home. Men, however, now had to rely on their wives, and in some cases their children to provide income to keep their families together. Many husbands lost their self-respect and, in desperation, left their families. Unfortunately, thousands of families broke up (one 1940 study showed that approximately 1.5 million married women were abandoned by their husbands). Many millions of families, however, stayed together and somehow got through those difficult years.

On the other hand, tragic stories were not uncommon during those times. Many, many women had just too much to do – too much to handle. Women, it seems, had to have four hands to do everything that needed to be done – and in countless ways they did. They were constantly cooking, baking, washing, gardening, jarring, sewing and playing doctor to all the kids. The millions of stories of these courageous women, who sacrificed so much to keep their families together, will never be told. It was the fabric of these women that held their families together. These invisible women are now all gone, but they should not be forgotten.

Following the market crash in 1929, wages decreased steadily for women who worked in industry and continued to be low for women throughout the Depression. Since separate statistics were not kept for unemployed women at that time, it is difficult to determine how many women were actually unemployed.

Many young women who graduated from high school as valedictorians or salutatorians did not have the opportunity to further their education. Too often, they went to work in a factory or got married. Some who attended business school also performed very well there. The few that had the means to go to college always ended up on the Dean's Honor Roll.

52. This has been home for three years.

Migrant Mother

Dorothea Lane was a photographer who worked for the Resettlement Administration (later called the Farm Security Administration) during the Great Depression. She ended up taking one of the most iconic photos of the era.

Dorothea and her husband, Paul Taylor, worked together documenting the exploitation of sharecroppers and migrant workers. Paul, who was a professor of economics, collected economic data while Dorothea took photos.

53. Dorothea Lange at work.

In the early spring of 1936, Dorothea was traveling alone in the field for a month taking photos of migratory farm workers in California. When her work was finished, she packed up her gear and started on her long trip home. It was a rainy day in March as Dorothea drove along the highway when she noticed a small crude sign that read "pea-pickers camp."

Though she had already taken many photos, when she was some 20 miles past the little sign on the side of the road she suddenly made a U-turn and headed back to the pea-pickers camp. When she arrived at the rainy campsite, she met a mother with her three children.

Dorothea Lange wrote:

She said that they had been living on frozen vegetables from the surrounding fields, and birds that the children killed. She had just sold the tires from her car to buy food. There she sat in that lean-to tent with her children huddled around her, and seemed to know that my pictures might help her, and so she helped me. There was a sort of equality about it.

The San Francisco News used several of Lange's pictures in an article featuring the poor, hungry, harvest workers who were living in filthy and miserable conditions.

One of the photos that did not appear in the news story was printed later that year in two other publications. The caption for the photo read, "Look in Her Eyes."

T. H. Watkins wrote:

Ultimately it would become one of the most famous and frequently published photographs in American History – "Migrant Mother," a Madonna-like image of a woman with haunted eyes, a hand at her mouth in worry, an infant in her lap, and two of her other children hiding their faces against her neck. For millions of Americans, it was and remains the living representation of the Great Depression.

The photo Dorothea Lange took on that rainy day at the pea-pickers camp of Florence Thompson, who had seven children, only took 10 minutes. It became one of the most famous and frequently published photos of the Depression.

54. The migrant mother.

The Model T

During the 1930s, there were a number of Model Ts running about in Big Mine Run – we called them "tin lizzies." They could be purchased from a junkyard for $20 or less. In most cases, the car was not in running order and had to be towed to the purchaser's home. Model Ts were simple in design and it wasn't too difficult to get them in running order again. If a guy bought a Model T from another person in our patch, there was no paper transaction, no owner's card, and no license plates, just cash for the car.

The Model T had a crank insert located at the front of the car near the bottom of the radiator. Someone (usually an older person) would crank the car to get it started while the driver would be at the controls. It usually took several turns of the crank to get the engine started. Sometimes the crank handle would quickly turn in the opposite direction, and if you didn't release the handle fast enough you could easily injure or break your wrist. So we were always told that whenever you cranked a car, you should never hold the crank handle with a normal grip. We were instructed to hold the crank with your hand and fingers, but to keep your thumb straight out and not in a clenched manner.

The guys who owned Model Ts were always working on the engine. It seemed that all they needed was a pair of pliers, a screwdriver or two and a set of adjustable wrenches to keep the car in running order.

The Model Ts were easy to drive and also inexpensive to operate. The owners didn't even need drivers' licenses. The guys drove their tin lizzies on all of the dirt roads in Big Mine run and nobody bothered them, and you could drive for some time on just one gallon of gasoline, which only cost 15 cents.

Flat tires were very common. After locating the hole and repairing the leak in the innertube, it was placed inside the tire. Then you had to pump it with a manually operated air pump and that was difficult to do. Sometimes the older guys would let us kids use the air pump to fill the tire, but it was very hard to do and they would just laugh when they saw how we struggled. We quickly learned that it took the strength of a grown-up to do the job satisfactorily.

55. A 1925 Model T Runabout.

The 1925 Model T Runabout in the photo was the most popular Model T in Big Mine Run. We got free rides by sitting in the rear. The driver would go around turns very fast and sometimes he would attempt to climb a seep hill even though there was no road. On occasion, one of the kids would actually fall out of the Model T because the driver made too many fast turns. I was scared a few times when riding in the rear because there wasn't anything to hold on to.

From 1908 to 1927, Henry Ford had sold over 15 million Model Ts. It was arguably America's favorite car for many decades. The Model T was like the "little red caboose" that could.

Minersville and the Supreme Court

It was 1935 and I was 11 years old. I was in the sixth grade in a one-room school building in Big Mine Run. When the school bell rang we all took our seats. The teacher asked for silence and motioned for all of us to stand. We all stood (as we did every day), recited the Pledge of Allegiance and saluted the American flag.

On a similar fall day in October 1935, Lillian Gobitas (age 12) and her brother William (age 10) went to public school in Minersville, which was about 15 miles from our home. On that day, William refused to recite the Pledge of Allegiance and salute the flag. The next day, Lillian also refused to say the pledge of Allegiance and salute the flag. The Gobitas children did not comply with the school's policy because they were Jehovah's Witnesses and believed in the Old Testament's prohibition against graven images and idolatry. After several weeks of discussion, the matter was not resolved satisfactorily and the school board expelled the two children.

56. William and Lillian Gobitas with their father shortly after being expelled from school.

The *Shenandoah Evening Herald*, Oct. 16, 1935:

Two Minersville Pupils
Refuse To Salute Flag

By Morey J. Potter
United Press Correspondent

Harrisburg, Oct. 16. (U.P.) – Whether Pennsylvania public school students should be forced to salute the American flag is discretionary to local school officials, the United Press was told today by W. M. Denison, counsel on school law for the State Department of Public Instruction.

His comment was prompted by three refusals reported this month, an unprecedented number as compared to the four previously handled by the department in the last decade.

Denison revealed he was asked for advice this week on two refusals to salute the flag, reported by C.E. Roudabush, superintendent of the Minersville schools.

Walter, the father, was a hard working son of Lithuanian immigrants. At the time, Walter operated a grocery store in Minersville. Since many of his customers were unemployed, he allowed them to purchase groceries on credit. Nevertheless, many people in the town viewed the rebellious behavior of the Gobitas children to be un-American, and Walter's family felt the anger of the town.

Walter was hoping that his children would be reinstated in school. The problem regarding the Pledge of Allegiance and flag salute, however, deteriorated and eventually ended up in the court. The case was held in a district court in Philadelphia. Somewhat surprisingly to many, the judge ruled in favor of the Gobitas children. The Minersville School board then appealed the decision to the United States Supreme Court. In 1940, the Supreme Court overturned the decision of the District Court in favor of the Minersville School Board.

Then, in 1943, The Supreme Court took on another flag-salute case in West Virginia, which again involved the children of Jehovah's Witnesses being expelled for not complying with school policy. In a landmark decision, the Supreme Court reversed its earlier decision.

During the eight-year period of legal proceedings, the Gobitas children had been attending a school, which the Jehovah's Witnesses started for their own students. Following the 1943 Supreme Court decision, the Minersville School Board invited the Gobitas children back to school. By this time, Lillian was 20-years-old and William was 18; they were both working at the family store. It was now too late for them to complete their public school education, so they never received a high school diploma. The Supreme Court ruling did, however, benefit the younger Gobitas children as well as the children of all other Jehovah's Witnesses. They were now able to return to public school and were no longer required to recite the Pledge of Allegiance or salute the flag.

In 1945, William Gobitas left Minersville and for the next 10 years did missionary work. Then he worked for the Maryland Casualty Company in Milwaukee and retired as personnel manager in 1976. He also worked for a number of years as a piano tuner in Wisconsin. He died in 1989 at the age of 64.

Lillian also left Minersville that same year and worked for seven years at the World Headquarters of Jehovah's Witnesses in Brooklyn. While attending a religious ceremony in Germany in 1952, she met Erwin Klose, a Jehovah's Witness who had been arrested a number of times by the German Secret Police during World War II. Lillian and Erwin married in Vienna in 1954. Later they moved to Atlanta, Ga., where they reared two children, Stephen and Judith.

The *Shenandoah Evening Herald,* June 6, 1940:

Two William Penn Colliery Employees Quit Their Jobs; Refuse To Salute The Flag

Two William Penn Colliery employees voluntarily relinquished their jobs this morning in preference to saluting the American flag, which was hoisted above the mineshaft.

A spokesman for the mine committee announced that Charles Billman, Shenandoah, and John Walaitis, Frackville, were the only ones of approximately 300-day shift employees who ignored the request to raise their hands in salute.

Given their choice of either saluting the flag or quitting their jobs, the two men decided to go home. The committee spokesman said both would get their jobs back when "they change their minds."

The action to request employees to salute Old Glory was prompted after the mine committee and superintendent received numerous complaints from employees that they will refuse to work aside of any man who does not pledge allegiance to the American flag.

"With so many complaints we decided it would be necessary to weed out all those who are adverse to the American principles," the committee spokesman declared.

The two men are members of Jehovah's Witnesses, a group which believes flag salting violates the second of the Ten Commandments – prohibiting worship of images.

Night shift employees, totaling about 150, will also be asked to salute the flag. The mine committee is expecting more refusals, in view of the fact that several other employees are known to be members of the sect.

In connection with the developments at William Penn Colliery, Walitis and Billman called at the Evening Herald office his morning to present their side of the issue.

Both men said they expected such action would result but wished to emphasize the fact that they are good Americans and said that one doe not have to salute the flag to be a good American.

Walitis said he served n France with the famous First Division, A. E. F., and saw action in six battles. Billman was too young to serve in the war, he said. Both men said they are native-born Americans and in setting forth their objection to saluting the flag, asserted that: "We serve God's Commandments first regardless of what the opposition is." By this statement, they meant that it is contrary to their religious beliefs to salute any images.

They added that under no circumstances would they salute the flag or worship any image "even if it means death."

The *Shenandoah Evening Herald*, June 7, 1940:

TWO MORE GIVE UP JOBS AT WILLIAM PENN MINE

Two more William Penn Colliery employees preferred to give up their jobs rather than salute the American flag atop the mineshaft.

Clarence Billman Jr., Shenandoah Heights, was the only member of the second shift yesterday to ignore the request of the mine committee and company officials while William Tlumacki, Lost Creek, did likewise on the third shift.

The former is a brother of Charles Billman, who along with Charles Walaitis, refused to salute the flag yesterday morning.

Employees were not expected to salute the flag today. Meanwhile, the future action of the four men was not disclosed. However, the mine committee insisted that employees would refuse to work with any man who did not pledge allegiance to the flag.

Having Babies

During the Depression, many women who had babies gave birth at home. There was no money for a hospital bill and some women couldn't even afford to pay a doctor's fee. Additionally, many women chose to have an abortion (which was illegal) because they couldn't afford children.

Some women attempted to abort their pregnancies by themselves; others went to non-professionals. In both cases abortions were often botched and ended in permanent injury and even death. During the Depression, approximately 5,000 deaths were blamed on botched abortion attempts each year.

Penicillin and other antibiotics, which would have reduced the risks of abortion, did not become available until World War II. Women of means could afford professional care if they chose to have an abortion performed, but poor women (in most cases) could only receive non-professional and potentially dangerous assistance if they were to have an abortion.

"The Angel of Ashland" Dr. Robert Spencer, a competent Ashland, Pa. physician, did an unbelievable thing during the Depression. By his own admission, he performed thousands of illegal abortions. The women who came to Dr. Spencer for an abortion did not have clandestine appointments in shabby apartments or sleazy motel rooms. They received excellent medical care and they were treated with respect. Furthermore, Dr. Spencer's fees were modest; he did not take advantage of these women who desperately needed professional medical help.

Wealthy, middle class and poor women all sought his services. Dr. Spencer's name and reputation were widely known. Women from all over Pennsylvania and beyond came to him. Vincent Genovese's book, *The Angel of Ashland*, details the life and work of Dr. Spencer.

57. Dr. Robert Spencer.

I was quite familiar with the location of Dr. Spencer's office and clinic – I walked by it many, many times. When I was only a youngster, I did look at his office as I strolled by because of "talk" I heard of what went on in his office. Later, when I understood what was going on in his clinic I just discretely walked by and did not even look at his office.

He was often called upon to perform difficult operations other physicians could not do.

The Ashland Daily News, May 3, 1933:

Pin Is Removed From Larynx of 13-Year-Old Girardville Child

A straight pin, lodged in the larynx of 13-year-old Veronica Burnatis of Girardville, was removed last night by Dr. R. D. Spencer at his office here and the child was none the worse for her experience today.

She swallowed the pin last Saturday while playing with her infant sister. She complained shortly afterward of pain in her mouth and throat and when her condition became worse Dr. Bronson of Girardville, was summoned and he ordered the removal of the child to Ashland State Hospital.

It was at first thought the pin was lodged in the girl's mouth but more minute examination revealed it in her larynx. Last night she was brought from the hospital to the office of Dr. Spencer here where the operation was successfully performed.

Dr. Spencer used a Laryngoscope and Laryngeal grasping forceps to extricate the pin. The child's ability to talk, which was practically taken away by the pin, was partly restored today and she will completely recover her voice as soon as the irritation caused by the presence of the pin heals.

Hard times and social problems tend to go together. Studies show that early in the Depression up to one million abortions were being carried out yearly in the United States. It was a sharp increase from the prosperous 1920s. Furthermore, the number of abortions increased during the entirety of the 1930s.

In the '30s, the number of births also dropped sharply and the population increased by only 7 percent, whereas the population increased by about 16 percent in the previous decade. Many young people delayed getting married. Furthermore, the divorce rate dropped sharply; it was too costly to pay attorney's fees as well as financially supporting two households. Tragically, suicides also increased from 1929 to 1930 and then remained high through the decade.

Mealtime

58. Big sister preparing a meal.

For the most part, I think we ate reasonably well. We didn't have meat very often; when we did eat meat it was usually bologna, chicken or hamburger. Mom told us that she ate meat only once or twice a year as a young girl growing up in Poland.

We were told to eat everything that was on our plate, whether we liked it or not, (that was probably a standard line heard by millions of youngsters during those times). We soon learned not to complain about the food. We ate it, and that was that. There were no special dishes prepared for anyone in addition to the main meal.

When I was about 8 years old I would play with other kids in a large sand pile near the railroad that went to the Bast Colliery. Later in the afternoon, after we got tired of playing, another youngster and I would walk along the railroad tracks toward the Colliery. Then we would sit on the railroad tracks and wait for the coal miners as they walked home from work.

All the miners carried a lunch pail or lunch box. As they walked by, we would ask if they had any leftovers. Sometimes we would get half of a sandwich, a piece of fruit or a piece of cake. Of course, we were always hoping for cake or pie. If they didn't have anything, they would often show us that their lunch box was empty. Just imagine, after working hard all day the miners took time to be nice to us – they were never rude.

Many people in small towns and rural areas raised chickens during those times. We not only raised chickens, but also ducks. When poor families kicked a chicken, many of them used the whole thing, including the feathers. I recall Mom boiling the feet of a chicken, which she then ate. I couldn't stand the sight of those damn chicken feet and I don't know how she ate them.

I now wonder how many mothers ate boiled chicken feet so their children could eat the good parts of the chicken, and how many parents ate less food during those times so their children had more.

59. It's time to eat.

We didn't have too many "store bought" cakes or pies. For the most part, we had homemade desserts. We did, however, always have applesauce; there were times when I just got tired of eating applesauce. Mom didn't bake many desserts, but she did make apple pies, and I'm ashamed to say so, but there also were times when I was looking for another kind of pie. Sometimes when we visited relatives or friends I would get a "store bought" dessert and that was always a nice treat. We had various flavors of homemade jelly on-hand at our house, but we rarely had peanut butter to go along with it. When I got hungry for a snack, I could always rely on a good old-fashioned jelly sandwich.

60. A child in the front yard in Natchez, Mississippi (ca. 1935).

Stealing Milk

Joe Baldino, who was reared with 11 other siblings, often went hungry and seldom got any milk to drink at home. In those days a milkman delivered milk in glass containers to individual homes. He would simply leave the quart milk bottle on the customer's front porch or doorstep. Joe noticed that people didn't always take in the bottle of milk as soon as it was delivered and he would casually walk over to the front porch, reach down and remove the small round cardboard lid on top of the bottle and take a sip or two of milk (not too much) and place the bottle back down. In cold weather, the frozen cream on top would actually push the small cardboard lid upward and off the bottle. The small frozen cylinder-shaped cream would be about an inch high. Joe would reach down and help himself to the frozen cream portion, put the lid back on and nonchalantly walk away. When Joe was telling me this story, he was laughing because he said the frozen cream was "a helluva lot better" than just plain milk.

The *Shenandoah Evening Herald*, Sept. 4, 1931:

THREE YOUTHS ARRESTED FOR STEALING MILK

Three local youths operating a Nash touring car were arrested by operators of the Kane detective agency, of Shamokin, yesterday afternoon on charges of stealing milk bottles from porches at Shenandoah Heights.

The boys were driving an unlicensed automobile and were taking milk from every porch along the street, and almost ran over three residents of the heights who attempted to stop the car and the occupants.

Detectives from the Shamokin agency came into town yesterday and placed the youths under arrest. They were taken before Justice A. M. Walukewicz, where the case was settled by payment of costs of the milk stolen and the Justices fees.

The *Shenandoah Evening Herald*, Dec. 4, 1931:

SHOT WHILE STEALING MILK FROM PORCH

John Kalidas is in the Locust Mountain State Hospital suffering from a bullet wound of the thigh, which he is alleged to have received when caught in the act of stealing milk bottles from porches on White Street this morning.

Police Chief John Mahr, who is investigating the shooting, stated that he did not know who shot the man, but it is very evident that he was one of the milk thieves that have been operating in Shenandoah during the last few mornings.

Recently, local milk dealers reported the theft of a large quantity of milk from porches in various sections of the community. Residents who have been victims of the thief or thieves are said to have fixed a trap for the milk robber and it is believed that Kalidas met some person who was waiting for the thief to appear.

As high as 20 and 30 quarts of milk have been stolen in one morning, it was said, and residents and milk dealers have organized to protect their property. Police believe the shooting of Kalidas will put an end to milk thefts in town.

The *Shenandoah Evening Herald*, May 16, 1935:

4 MORE YOUTHS HELD FOR STEALING MILK

Four Morea youths are held for court following their arrest on charges of stealing milk from porches of homes throughout the Mahanoy Valley. The quartet were arraigned before Squire Joseph Sweeney at Girardville and held under $300 bail each.

As high as 20 quarts of milk have disappeared from porches in one morning at Gilberton and Mahanoy Plane. The dairy proprietors point out that the dairy company not only suffers the loss of the bottles, but the consumer suffers the loss of the milk. The inconvenience caused the residents of the Mahanoy Valley resulted in their appeal to the dairy companies to make an investigation. Today's arrests are expected to be followed by others. The Kane detectives have been engaged to patrol the routes of both dairy companies.

Denise Wietry, evening supervisor of the circulation desk at Shippensburg University, told me that her mother was explaining how difficult it was to live through the 1930s. Joanne Lane, Denise's mother, who was reared in Huntingdon County, in south central Pennsylvania, told her daughter that she ate lard and onion sandwiches as a young girl (it probably was "better tasting" than just a plain lard sandwich, which some people also ate during the Depression). A syrup sandwich or a plain slice of bread with sugar sprinkled on top was childrens' favorites.

Wanda Kehler Edelman, my classmate at Butler Township High School, told me about her family eating lettuce sandwiches. Indeed, many families back then ate that kind of sandwich because they were cheap to prepare. You simply go out to the vegetable garden and cut off the lettuce tops. Then you take the lettuce into the kitchen (sometimes wash it) and put it between two slices of bread. Can you imagine how many sales McDonalds would make if they offered a plain lettuce sandwich?

Our family, like many others, bought some groceries at our neighborhood store. Jacob Bielarski had a small grocery store in Woodland Heights and that's where we bought bread, bologna, milk and other small items. We generally bought one item at a time and only what we needed. We made those purchases "on tick," or "on account," which meant on credit. Another way of saying it was, "on account of the fact that we had no money."

Our grocery bill was about five or six dollars every two weeks. My family usually allowed me to go to the grocery store to pay our grocery bill, because after I paid it, the grocer always gave me a small bag of penny candy.

Hunting and Fishing

During the various hunting seasons, men and young lads went hunting for rabbits, pheasants and deer. It was an important source of food for many families. I recall stories about men who also went hunting out of season for animals like deer. It was illegal, but a practical way of helping to feed one's family. It was a similar situation with fishing; it brought in much-needed food.

My father did not go hunting or fishing. One day our neighbor gave my Mom a rabbit he shot. I was asked or told at our evening meal to just taste a small piece, but I couldn't do it. I kept thinking about that poor rabbit. We also had other neighbors who would also share some fish they caught or a pheasant they shot. They were just as poor as we were, but neighbors often shared what little they had with each other. It was not unusual to see poor people helping other poor people.

Soup and More Soup

61. Children in a soup line.

People always said Mom was a good cook. When she came to America as a young woman she worked as a cook in several well-known restaurants in Philadelphia; during the Depression, the scarcity of food played an important part in her becoming an even better cook.

During the Depression, people who had a back yard or some other available space had a vegetable garden. We planted lettuce, onions, potatoes, tomatoes, cucumbers, carrots, cabbage, beans, red beets and a few other things. And many of those vegetables ended up in soup.

Mom made soup every day. I recall that she also made a soup with milk, which had small dough balls in it.

She often prepared her own noodles. She made her own dough, which she smoothed out with a rolling pin until it looked like a large pancake. The dough was then folded several times. She would hold her fingers very close to the edge of the folded dough and began cutting down swiftly with a sharp knife, cutting off nicely shaped noodles. I was always afraid that she was going to cut herself. When she was done (with all of her fingers intact), the noodles were all about the same size – almost as if they had been cut by a machine. Sadly, I never realized how good Mom's noodle soup was until I grew older and ate commercially prepared noodle soup from a can. Some seven decades later, I still eat soup every day.

Sometimes we would crush crackers and put them in a cup of coffee. Since we ate it with a spoon, we called it "coffee soup." I was never too fond of coffee as a youngster, so I wasn't a big fan of coffee soup.

A number of people told me about another kind of soup they made called "ketchup soup." They simply took a ketchup bottle and poured some in hot water–that was it. Some desperate, hungry people would use the "free" ketchup that was on the counter or table in a diner.

Many people who lived in small towns and rural areas, as I mentioned earlier, had a vegetable garden. Those living in urban areas where they didn't have vegetable gardens had a more difficult time feeding their families. One only has to look at pictures of long lines outside soup kitchens, which were common in the cities, to see how desperate it was.

Soup was quite economical, since water could be added to the large pots to make more. In some major cities, several thousand people could be served in just one day.

Making "Bums' Soup"

We got the idea to make our own bums' soup from our visits to the hobo camp where we saw them making soup. At that time in Big Mine Run we referred to the hobos as bums, so the soup we saw them making became "bums' soup" to us. Each of us went home to see if we could find a potato, onion or carrot. George Mickel, who suggested the idea, brought a small pot of water and a knife. The rest of us brought a cup and a spoon.

We marched off to the woods a short distance away and built a fire. The veggies we had were peeled, cut, and boiled.

The fire that we made was probably too large because we had plenty of wood available and kept feeding it. We all sat around and watched as the soup came to a boil. Then we all took turns tasting it to see if it was done. When we finally decided that the soup was ready to eat, we all had a cup. As you may have guessed, we all said it was good; we all lied. I never felt that our bums' soup was as good as Mom's, but I kept that to myself. I suppose the other kids kept that secret to themselves, too.

Jarring (Canning)

Since we had a garden we grew all kinds of vegetables, (even though my Mom was very busy, she still managed to grow different varieties of flowers around our house. She also kept many flowers in small red ceramic pots in different rooms throughout our home). We jarred them all. I helped to stuff small cucumbers into jars because my hands were small and could easily fit into them. Mom also made chow-chow and chili sauce, which we also jarred. We jarred peaches, pears and huckleberries and we made strawberry, peach and grape jellies.

We stored the jarred items on shelves in our basement. All throughout the winter, I was usually the one assigned to go to the basement to bring up a jar of chili sauce or a jar of something else. When I was asked to get a jar of jelly I always chose strawberry. I liked strawberry jelly sandwiches better than the others.

62. A typical basement with many jars of food.

One day Mom sent me to the basement to bring her some empty jars since she was putting up vegetables for the winter. As I reached down into a large basket of empty jars, I notice a small coin purse at the bottom of the basket. When I opened it, I was very surprised to see that the purse contained some folded paper money and some coins. I quickly ran upstairs and gave it to her. She was excited and very happy. It was the purse she had lost about a week ago and felt that it was lost forever. Apparently, it accidentally fell from her bosom when she bent over as she worked in the basement. The purse contained eight dollars and some change. Mom gave me a big hug, said I was a good little boy, and gave me a nickel as a reward. I felt good that I was able to do something to make her happy. I went up to my bedroom and put the nickel in my small coin box where I also had a few pennies saved.

The Late Mid-1930s

FDR's First Term

63. Sharecroppers' families with their children.

During FDR's first term in office, the Supreme Court struck down a number of his New Deal programs. In May 1935, the Court declared both the National Industrial Recovery Act (NIRA) and six months later the Agricultural Adjustment Administration (AAA) unconstitutional. The NIRA allowed American Industrialists to collaborate to set prices of products and also the wages of employees; the AAA was designed to relieve the economy by increasing purchasing power – especially the power of farmers. It was to help farmers by reducing production of some crops, thereby stabilizing farm prices and encouraging more diversified farming.

By the latter part of FDR's first term in office, the country was still in a depression. His New Deal policies were easing hard times for many people, but the economy was still not doing well. While the government's massive spending helped ease the economic crisis, it did not end it. There simply weren't enough jobs, and by July 1935, unemployment was still very high, at 21 percent.

64. A 13-year-old sharecropper.

The *Shenandoah Evening Herald,* Jan. 31, 1935:

RELIEF FUNDS EXHAUSTED STATE SITUATION SERIOUS

Harrisburg, Jan. 31 (U.P.) – The State Emergency Relief Board, needing $20,902,750 for February allocations, is facing the most critical financial period in the two years of its existence.

The general fund is empty. The federal government has not made a February allocation. An agreement between Governor H. Earle and Harry L. Hopkins, federal relief administrator, is awaited.

Consequently, the board at its monthly meeting yesterday went through the formality of designating specified amounts for various forms of relief during the next month, subject to the receipt of funds.

65. Georgia woman sorting tobacco.

Meanwhile, Robert L. Johnson, executive secretary of the board, has undertaken a complete reorganization of county board units. He has announced the resignations of relief board members in at least 11 counties. Some were requested; others were voluntary.

The *Shenandoah Evening Herald,* July 25, 1936:

1789 FAMILIES HERE ARE WITHOUT RELIEF

The county's relief clients, including 1,789 in the Shenandoah district, will be on extremely limited diet this week-end while hoping that relief orders, already several days overdue, will be coming through again next week.

Fear that actual starvation might result when meager food provisions in the home of the relief dependents are exhausted, has been reduced by the fact that many grocers are "carrying" these unfortunates with a hope that they will be paid when the state Legislature provides more money for the purpose.

Cessation of food orders is accompanied by a curtailment of the medical and dental assistance program, but it is generally assumed that the doctors will continue to treat patients on relief during the present emergency.

Paradoxically, the list of relief applicants at present is higher than at any time within the past year. The Shenandoah district, which includes the borough, West Mahanoy Township, Frackville, Ringtown, Gilberton, and Ashland, is one of the biggest districts in the county. Shenandoah alone has 831 families on the relief rolls.

66. Bud Fields and family in Alabama.

After School

Shortly after walking home from grade school, I would change from my school clothes to some older clothing. There were no snacks, no radio, no other musical gadgets to listen to and, of course, no TV or computers before our evening meal. If I had any chores to do, I did those first.

Then I went looking for coal up on the hill behind our home, which had many coal holes. When my 100-pound bag was full, I would haul it home on my homemade wheelbarrow.

After our evening meal, I would always get started on my homework. I did not play outside very much during schooldays. And I usually went to bed by nine o'clock.

Youngsters today are dismissed from school much earlier than we were. So when kids come home from school today, they might have a snack (today's' homes are generally well-supplied), open up their computer, use their cell phone or iPod. Later when they do their homework, they might also be listening to music at the same time. They also do a lot of communicating with each other (text messaging and so on). I feel sure that they are going to bed much later than I did.

With technology moving ahead as rapidly as it does, it taxes the mind to try to think of what the next several generations of students will do after school.

When the Junkman Came Around

One of the few ways I was able to earn a little money for myself was to collect scrap items, which I sold to the "junkman." The junkman drove a large open truck and once every two weeks he would roll slowly through Woodland Heights. As he drove by, he would ring a fairly loud bell and call out, "any old rags, old junk, old iron!"

Mom made braided rugs, and she always had small pieces of cloth left over. I would stuff those pieces into a large cloth bag. I also gathered any other old clean rags I found lying about and put them in my ragbag.

I also collected various kinds of metal that I knew the junkman would buy. Whenever I found a piece of scrap iron lying about, I would pick it and haul it home. The junkman paid the least amount of money per pound for iron since it was more plentiful than other metals. I knew the price per pound I would get for aluminum, brass, copper and iron. I collected all these different metals and kept them in small piles since the junkman weighed each pile separately.

When I had enough junk to sell, I would wave for the junkman to stop. He carried a small brass scale with a hook on the bottom to weigh my bag of rags. When I had a sufficient amount of a particular metal, he would put it in a cloth bag and weigh it. If I only had a relatively small amount of metal, he would simply offer me a price without weighing it.

I generally earned between 20 and 30 cents for my junk. On a good day, I would make as much as 50 cents. I always showed my Mom what I earned and, of course, she always allowed me to keep my earnings.

When the Peddlers Came Around

The kids in Big Mine Run, including myself, always enjoyed peddlers when they came selling their services or other "stuff." We would follow them as they went from house to house, because they always walked and did not have a vehicle. While they were somewhat strange-looking, they were always friendly.

The "umbrella man" came around fixing and selling umbrellas. And he would be carrying his umbrellas in a backpack of some sort. He always sang out some song-like message describing his umbrella services.

The "scissors man" also was a regular peddler. He sharpened scissors, knives and other small tools. He also sold a variety of scissors. And as he walked about, he called out in a song-like manner describing his services.

Making Braided Rugs

67. My Mom's braided rug looked like this.

Mom made beautiful braided rugs. She started by cutting strips of cloth about one-half inch wide from all kinds of colored clothing. The strips, which were various lengths, were sewn end-to-end to make one long, multi-colored strip. This long strip was wound around itself until it became a ball about the size of a cantaloupe.

Then she would take the individual strips from three balls and make them into a tightly wrapped braid. Mom used a large sewing needle and waxed thread as she began hand sewing the braid to make a rug. She made both round and oval rugs, which were about one-half inch thick. Her eyesight wasn't too good, so she always asked me to thread her needle so she could continue sewing.

When I was a young kid, I would sit on the floor and play with the extra cloth balls she had on hand in her large sewing basket. Sometimes I would partially unravel one because I would play too roughly with it, but Mom never scolded me. She would just reach down, pick up the ball and wrap it up again, and then hand it to me.

She was pleased when she completed a rug. Then she would place it on the floor for us to walk on. I was always reluctant to walk on a rug that she just made with my shoes because they were beautiful and required a lot of work. So I just took off my shoes and walked on the rug in my stocking feet.

One day when I was a little older, I put several of Mom's braided rugs away. I didn't want any one to walk on them. Now, seven decades later, they look just as they did back in the 1930s when she finished them. They are unique and I treasure them – made by my Mom's very busy, busy hands. Now, when I look at them, I am both happy and sad.

Store at Your Door

Convenience stores are common today. It's not unusual for a small town to have several of them. We simply get into our cars and drive to a nearby convenience store to make our purchases.

During the 1930s in Big Mine Run and most other places, however, we actually had convenience stores and vendors that practically came to our front doors. Farmers came with all kinds of produce, bakery truck drivers delivered bread and baked goods, milkmen delivered milk, the iceman delivered ice and we even had a store on wheels with groceries (a *very* convenient store) stop in front of our home.

About once every two weeks, a truck as big as a medium-sized moving van would come through Woodland Heights. The sign on the truck read: STORE AT YOUR DOOR, and that's exactly what it was. It contained all kinds of day-to-day groceries that a family needed. At the time, it was a novel way to sell groceries and the mobile store received a lot of attention.

When the truck stopped in front of our home, I would accompany my mother on her shopping trip. We stepped inside at the rear of the truck, which had an area big enough for several customers to gaze at the merchandise. Every available space in the truck was filled with canned goods, luncheon meat and groceries of all kinds.

The driver was also the grocer. His name was Joe Morris and he operated the truck for his father, who had a grocery store business in Girardville about two miles from Big Mine Run. When we were done shopping I always carried the bagged groceries from the truck to our home.

The Beginning of FDR's Second Term

In November 1936, FDR defeated Alfred Landon, governor of Kansas, for the presidency by a convincing 532-8 electoral vote. It was Roosevelt's second straight landside victory.

68. A long line of unemployment men, N. Y.

The *Shenandoah Evening Herald*, Nov. 14, 1936:

ROOSEVELT SWEEPS NATION CARRIES 46 STATES;

NEW DEAL POLICIES OKAYED BY PEOPLE.

In January 1937, however, unemployment was still 15 percent. It increased to 18.9 percent by December. Clearly, the economy was still weak. Nevertheless, Roosevelt was confident and charismatic. He spoke with such compassion that the American people trusted him. He gave the common man at the bottom of the economic pyramid hope – hope that things would get better.

69. Families of evicted sharecroppers, 1936.

In his inauguration speech, FDR said, "I see one-third of a nation ill-housed, ill-clad and ill-nourished." The president knew that he still had much to do. He felt that his second landslide reelection, however, gave him a mandate to press forward with additional reforms in an attempt to improve the economy.

FDR pushed for what he called judicial efficiency. He remembered and was still annoyed that the Supreme Court had struck down some New Deal programs in his first term. He felt that the majority members of the Court were both political and obstructionist.

In February 1937, he proposed a bold new legislative act titled, "The Judiciary Reorganization Bill," which gave the president the power to expand the number of justices on the Supreme Court to create a sympathetic majority.

70. Evicted from her home, now on the street.

As it turned out, opposition to FDR's bill came from all sides. The bill was viewed as an attempt to stack the court and soon became known as the "Court-packing plan." Congress did not support the president and his proposed legislation failed. It was a major defeat for FDR. The political consequences went beyond his attempt to reform the Supreme Court. He not only lost his bipartisan support in Congress, but his highly favorable opinion by the general public was somewhat diminished.

71. Advertising an evacuation sale.

The Victrola

Before we had a radio, we listened to music on a Victrola, which was a trademark name for a phonograph or record-playing machine. Our Victrola was about 3½ feet high and 1½ feet square.

There was a small crank on the upper right hand side, which was turned for a minute or so to power-up the record player. After placing a record on the turntable a short arm-like device with a needle at the end was set upon the record and the music began. If nobody remembered to crank up the Victrola, the turntable would slow to a stop. Someone would quickly jump up and crank the handle to get the music going again

72. This is what our Victrola looked like.

Many of our records were lively polka dance music. Other records were recordings of Ukrainian singers. We had no records of popular music.

Listening to the Radio

I was about 11-years-old when we bought our first radio. I can still remember how excited we all were when the deliveryman brought it to our home. It was a floor model about four feet high with a highly varnished wood-simulated finish. The front of the radio had a round-lighted dial with several control knobs.

We usually listened to the radio in the evenings, and in the beginning, everything we heard was exciting and entertaining. We kept turning the dial to get one radio station after another. Most of the time we didn't turn on the light in the room to save on the electrical bill; the dial on the radio provided enough light.

I often sat on the floor next to the radio listening to exciting programs like "Gang Busters," "The Shadow," "The Lone Ranger" and "Inner Sanctum Mysteries." When a radio station did not come in loud and clear, I would put my head next to the speaker to listen.

My sisters enjoyed listening to music. Their favorite radio program was "Your Hit Parade," which played the top 10 songs of the week. We all listened to family programs like the "Jack Benny Show," the "Charlie McCarthy Program" and the "Amos n' Andy Show," which was enjoyed by presidents Hoover and Roosevelt.

The most exciting and famous single radio reproduction of all time was broadcast on Oct. 30, 1938. I was 14 years old and just happened to be listening to the radio by myself that evening. Orson Welles did a broadcast called "War of the Worlds," about a Martian landing in New Jersey. The program was done in a realistic format and created panic and struck terror into the hearts of many throughout the country. It was no laughing matter – many who heard the terrifying program believed it, including me.

The *New York Daily News*, Oct. 31, 1938;

"FAKE RADIO 'WAR' STIRS TERROR THROUGH U. S."

The New York Times, Oct. 31, 1938:

"RADIO LISTENERS IN PANIC, TAKING WAR DRAMA AS FACT"

The broadcast, a Halloween trick, won Welles fame and notoriety, and is still talked about today.

Picking Huckleberries (Blueberries)

We picked huckleberries during the summer primarily to sell – it was one of the few ways to earn money. We also picked them to eat as dessert and for making pies, perogies and jelly. The berry-picking season lasted about three months.

Our entire family helped to pick huckleberries, but my sisters and I did most of the work because we had more time. We got up about five o'clock in the morning while it was still dark, and we would set out for the hills. We would often go without breakfast.

The early-morning dew made the bushes wet and it was cold and uncomfortable to walk through them. Since it was the summer we dressed lightly. Our sneakers and socks were soaked immediately, and we were wet from the waist down. We would continue to be wet and chilly until about eleven o'clock when the hot sun would dry things out. By noon, the sun would almost be too hot.

We always tied a one-quart container, which we called a picker, around our waists so we could pick berries with both hands. When the picker was full, we would empty the berries into a larger container that usually held about eight or 10 quarts.

On a good day, our entire family would pick about 25 or 30 quarts of berries. Since huckleberries were generally quite small, it took a while just to pick one quart. Also it took a lot of walking to find spots where the berries grew – they didn't grow everywhere. Often times the really great-looking patches of blueberry bushes had been picked clean by someone else. If you happened to find a place where the berries were plentiful and large, you called it a "kutch." You only revealed your kutch to family members or very good friends.

At the beginning of the berry-picking season we would get about 15 cents a quart. The price would continue to drop steadily throughout the summer, and by the end of the season we would only get 5 cents a quart. It was an early lesson in supply and demand. Today I pay about $3 for a quart for huckleberries. I still enjoy eating them.

Sometimes I would eat some of the berries while I was picking them, but we were politely reminded not to do that. Those berries were going to be sold. We always had plenty of berries to eat at home, but somehow they always tasted better when we were picking them. Huckleberry pie in the middle of the winter was a real treat.

Picking Mushrooms

My father enjoyed picking mushrooms and he was very good at it. He did not go out in the woods near our home, but he always took his car and drove to some place that he felt he would find better tasting mushrooms. Sometimes he would take me with him, but it was not something I liked to do.

He carried a 10-quart pail and a knife as he walked through the woods, and I would trail along a short distance behind him. He was quite knowledgeable about mushrooms and always looked for the small delicious ones rather than the more common varieties. Mushrooms grew in dark areas very close to the ground and often they were partially covered with dirt, leaves, moss and dead branches. Sometimes we would see snakes near to them. My father always managed to fill his large bucket with mushrooms before leaving to go home.

Frankly, I never showed any interest in picking them because I never ate them. Mushrooms never got any sunshine and they didn't appear to be food to me. It always surprised me to see how my family and many others enjoyed eating them. My Dad also shared the mushrooms he picked with neighbors, relatives and friends.

People said Mom made delicious mushroom soup, and I simply took their word for it. She also added mushrooms to the potato soup that she made. While I ate the potato soup, I never ate the mushrooms. It was the only thing I never ate at mealtime. My Mom also made dark brown gravy with mushrooms, which she used as a "topping" on other foods.

Sometimes she would thread mushrooms on a string about three feet long, which she would then make into a loop. After she had several loops, she would hang them behind our kitchen stove to dry. The dried mushrooms would be used in preparing future meals.

On occasion, my father would simply put some cleaned mushrooms on top of our kitchen coal stove and heat them on both sides. Then he would sprinkle salt on them and eat them like they were potato chips.

No matter how they were prepared, I said, "they're still mushrooms and I say to hell with them."

To tell the truth, I said that to myself.

Summer Vacation

As a youngster I spent some of my summers with my Uncle Bill Kuschick and his wife Mary who lived in Frackville, Pa. They didn't have any children of their own at the time.

Bill was a coal miner. He always had steady employment and so they were well-off compared to the average family. One day while working at the Repellier Colliery near Saint Clair, he accidentally cut off his thumb. He returned to work after surgery and a short rest.

Their home had indoor plumbing and a bathroom with a bathtub. That was a luxury for me; I always enjoyed taking baths when I stayed with them. In Big Mine Run we did not have running hot water in our home and we only had an outhouse.

Mary was a great cook and that was a good thing, because Bill loved good food. Of course that meant that I also ate well while I stayed with them. Bill always brought home a box of vanilla ice cream with cherries when he got paid.

I remember watching Mary peel potatoes once and telling her she was wasting a lot of potato by using a knife. I went on to tell her that my Mom used a potato peeler and only skimmed off the skin and hence didn't waste any potato. Mary laughed a little, but just kept on slicing. When Bill came home, she told him (in Russian) what I said about peeling potatoes (they often spoke to each other in Russian, which was Bill's native language). Since I spent a lot of time living with them, I could understand what they were saying when they spoke in Russian. Mary said it was unusual for a young kid to be aware of waste and frugality.

Bill liked dogs and I got to like them too. One of his dogs gave birth to a two-headed puppy once that caused some excitement. On another occasion he purchased a dog from somewhere in Illinois. When it arrived, it was like an addition to the family.

In the mid-1930s, Uncle Bill purchased a new Chevrolet coupe for $650. It was fun to ride in a new car, since most families had a used car if they had one at all. I recall him telling me that he had to drive the car at a modest speed for several hundred miles to "break it in." He also had a small fan installed on the dashboard to keep the windshield clear since cars did not have built-in defogging or air conditioning in them at the time.

They always treated me well and took me everywhere they went; some thought I was their child. Bill had a positive influence on me concerning the importance of an education.

At the end of the summer, they took me back home to Big Mine Run. Even though they were able to provide me with some material things, as well as taking good care of me, I was always pleased to be back home again.

73. FDR and Fala were inseparable.

The *Shenandoah Evening Herald*, Nov. 10, 1936:

Puppy Loves His Master Even If He's Plastered

Philadelphia. Nov. 10. (U.P.) – A small poodle dog that wanted to be with its master, whether he was drunk or sober, occupied a jail cell here today.

The other occupant of the cell, Lionel Phillips, 29, Chicago, the dog's owner, was accused of driving his automobile into a subway entrance. The poodle refused to desert Phillips, and wagged its tail happily when it was permitted to go to jail with him.

The *Shenandoah Evening Herald*, May 14, 1937:

OWNER OF KIDNAPED DOG AWAITS RANSOM LETTERS

St. Paul, Minn., May 14. (U.P.) – Eleven-year-old Edmar Fink choked back his tears today as he awaited ransom instructions from the kidnapers of Tippy, his Boston bull terrier.

Tippy, Edmar explained, had been his "pal" for a year and a half – ever since the dog was a month-old pup.

Several days go Tippy disappeared. Edmar was heart-broken. His parents, Mr. and Mrs. N. N. Fink, were reassuring. Surely an advertisement in the papers would result in the dog's return. The family offered a reward – all their modest income would permit.

Last night an anonymous telephone call was received at the Fink home.

"Your dog isn't lost," a man's voice said. "I have him and I'm holding him for ransom. It'll cost you $100 to get him back."

Edmar added up his assets: a ball glove, a collection of marbles and a bike.

"Gosh," he said. "I'd give 'em all to get Tippy back."

The *Shenandoah Evening Herald*, Aug. 12, 1940:

Boy Risks Own Life To Save His Dog 'Pal'

Wildwood, N.J. Aug. 12. (U.P.) – Thirteen-year-old Clair Bratton, of Philadelphia, risked his life to save his dog "Pal."

The boy and his dog, a Collie Spitz, were walking along the railroad trestle over a small lake here when he noticed a locomotive bearing down on them. William Buccuto, 24, of Philadelphia, a railroad watchman, shouted to Clair to jump from the bridge, saying he would rescue him from the lake.

Instead, Clair darted forward five feet, picked up his dog and then sprinted back toward the other end of the trestle. When he was within seven feet of safety the locomotive struck him and he fell, still hugging his dog, 25 feet into the water.

The dog, uninjured, swam ashore. Biccuto rescued Clair. His leg was broken.

A Depression Within a Depression

74. Housing near San Antonio, Texas.

In 1937 the economic picture was still bleak and stayed that way through most of 1938. Unemployment went from 14.3 percent in 1937 to 17.4 percent in January 1938. It simply appeared that the Depression would never end, and many people wondered if they were going to live their whole lives in poverty. All of this, despite the fact that FDR spent more money in his first five years in office than all 31 presidents before him combined.

In 1938 I was in the eighth grade in a one-room schoolhouse in Big Mine Run. Even though the country was still in a depression, we were a little better off than we were several years ago. By now my father was not able to work at all. My two older sisters, however, were employed in a shirt factory in Ashland and my Mom did housecleaning and laundry for three families. People everywhere were desperately hoping that the poor economic situation would soon turn around.

75. A family living behind a billboard in California.

The *Shenandoah Evening Herald*, Dec. 20, 1937:

OVER ONE-EIGHTH IN STATE ARE ON RELIEF ROLLS

Harrisburg, Dec. 20. (U.P.) – More than one-eighth of Pennsylvania's residents are public charges, State Assistant Secretary Karl de Schweinitz reported today as he went on trial before a "jury" of 35, accused of "wasteful and inefficient" administration of relief.

At the same time, the cabinet officer, whose $10,000-a-year job is at stake, reported the largest weekly increase in unemployment relief rolls since August, 1935, when WPA succeeded state work relief, and blamed curtailment of Federal works project employment largely for increasing jobless dole lists.

The report showed 1,264,000 public charges, more than one-eighth of the state's population, including the 487,202 direct relief recipients, 612,000 WPA workers, 95,000 on the old-age assistance rolls, 11,000 on blind pensions, 16,725 widows and 42,583 dependent children on the mothers' assistance files.

Figures for Schuylkill County included in the report were: Relief applications received, 322; cases on relief rolls, 5405; persons on relief rolls, 16,646; expenditures for direct relief, $34,982.80.

The Late 1930s

My Summer in a Coal Hole

My father and two of my uncles, John Skocick and Pete Daniels, operated a bootleg coal hole near Germantown about two miles from Big Mine Run. I started to go with my father to the coal hole during the summer months when I was about 14-years-old.

For the first week or so I helped Pete on the surface while my father and John went down inside the coalmine. Pete operated the cable car apparatus that controlled the car (called a buggy) that brought the coal to the surface from down inside the coal hole and lowered it back down again.

After several weeks I went down inside the coal mine, which at its deepest was several hundred feet below the ground. It was cool, damp and scary down there. Hacking at the coal was very hard, dangerous work. While I was down inside the coal hole, I could hear strange creaking and crunching noises, from time to time. Regular coal miners, I am told, quickly get accustomed to these noises, but they bothered me; I could almost feel the tons and tons of rock and coal over my head getting ready to come crashing down on top of me.

When John saw that I was not too pleased working down inside the coal mine, he gave me some advice. He said, "You can't work in a coal hole and be afraid. You must go down and do your job and that's that." While I liked and respected John, I did not want to do that kind of work for a living.

At the end of the summer, I had had enough with working in a coal hole. It motivated me more than anything else to get a good education. In the fall just before I entered high school I told Mom that I never wanted to work in a coal hole again. Apparently, she was able to persuade my father not to ask me to work in his coal hole again – thank God he never did.

Joe Baldino and the Donkey

Joe Baldino and I grew up in Big Mine Run during the 1930s. We became friends and did the things kids do living in a "patch." I left the coal region as a young lad and lost touch with Joe for many decades. After many years, I now e-mail or call him to talk about all those things we did in Big Mine Run during the Depression years.

Joe told me about his experience working in a coal hole one summer when he was about 15-years-old. His two older brothers, Tony and Leo, hired Joe for $1 a day.

The coal hole was called a "drift" or "tunnel" because it went straight on into the base of the mountain (Most bootleg coal holes were called slopes or inclines). A mine car, which rode on rails, was used to haul the coal from inside the tunnel. Joe helped to load the mine car and then it was his job to push the car to the outside of the coal hole.

76. From left, Leo and Joe Baldino.

One day his brother, Albert, who was the boss of the coal hole, reprimanded Joe for not working hard enough. Joe was assigned to cut timber for the coal hole. He was given an axe and a saw and sent up to the woods. Cutting timber and hauling it to the coal hole was very difficult work. Joe said he was so tired that evening when he got home that he fell asleep at the supper table.

Albert decided to buy a pony to pull the loaded coal car out of the mine. When the pony arrived at the Baldino home, Joe was allowed to ride the pony the relatively short distance to the coal hole.

When they arrived at the coal hole, the pony was hooked to the empty mine car. Joe led the pony several hundred feet into the tunnel to get loaded with coal. Unfortunately, the coal mine was too narrow at that point and they were unable to turn the pony around to pull out the loaded mine car. They had a difficult time getting the pony to back out of the mine all that distance.

They had to sell the pony back to the farmer from whom it was purchased. Sadly, not too long after that, Joe quit going to high school and went back to pushing the coal car back and forth inside the tunnel.

To this day, some seven decades later, my e-mail messages to him start with: "Coal Car Runner Joe."

77. A bootleg miner near Lykens, Pa., 1936.

Homemade Candy

I always enjoyed watching my sisters making homemade candy. The most popular candy they made was called "mozee;" it was made from molasses and sugar, which was heated to a rolling boil. After a while a small portion was removed with a teaspoon and put into a glass of cold water. My sisters allowed me to reach into the glass and take out the cooled candy to taste it. When it had a taffy-like consistency, it was done.

Then the heated mixture was poured into a buttered tin pie pan until it was about a quarter of an inch thick. If we had peanuts or coconut, we would sprinkle some on top and the candy was left to cool.

When it was ready we would break up the large round mozee into smaller portions and we would all have a piece. It was a very hard caramel that would soften and get chewy after you had it in your mouth for a while. It was not good for your teeth, but it was very tasty.

At Easter my sisters made white coconut Easter "eggs" as well as peanut butter eggs. After shaping the filling, they would dip each egg into hot dark chocolate and place them on wax paper to cool. After they were coated, the eggs were roughly the same size. I enjoyed the peanut butter eggs more than the coconut eggs. When I took a bite of an Easter egg and found it wasn't peanut butter, I would put it back with the others and help myself to another one. I was mildly reprimanded for doing that and was told to finish eating the egg I took and not put it back, but I wouldn't cooperate.

Sometimes my sisters would make fudge. Most of the time I couldn't wait for the fudge to harden and I would take a small piece while it was still warm and soft. Since I was the youngest in the family and the only boy, I was apparently allowed certain privileges.

Homemade Soda

One summer we bought a small bottle of root beer concentrate, followed the directions on the label and ended up making about five gallons of soda. I used a siphon hose, which was about the diameter of a ballpoint pen, to fill small bottles from the five-gallon container of soda. I had to be very careful to tightly squeeze the siphon hose with my thumb and index finger when each bottle was full so I could move the hose to the next one.

After filling about 30 bottles or so, I would place a metal cap on top of each. Then I would use a capper to clamp a metal cap on top of each bottle. Our homemade soda didn't taste exactly like store-bought soda, which we didn't get very often, but it was pretty good.

We also made our own grape soda from a grape juice concentrate. It was convenient to be able to go down to the basement to get a bottle of soda when we wanted a soft drink on a hot summer day.

Making Wine

I picked blackberries, elderberries and grapes so that Mom and I could make wine (my father never helped with these activities.) The blackberries and elderberries grew wild so they were free for the picking. Grapes were relatively cheap, but many families grew their own. We stored our three different homemade wines, which was mainly for our own use, in large wooden barrels.

We always had wine on hand for holidays and family visits. If I felt I was getting a cold or already had one, I would put some wine in hot tea and sip it slowly.

At times, however, we sold some wine in small bottles to our neighbors and friends. Our neighbor, James Monahan (who was a nice guy) liked our wine and he would stop in to talk and buy a small glass of wine for 10 cents. Mom was a generous person; even though she had very little herself, she always gave him a free glass of wine before he left.

Making Moonshine

The most interesting and exciting beverage we made was whiskey, which was called "moonshine" or "hooch." It was illegal to make it, but people didn't have money to purchase commercially made whiskey so they made their own.

I helped Mom make moonshine. It was not unusual for us to have 30 or 40 gallons of moonshine stored in wooden barrels in our basement. We always had a quart bottle of moonshine in our kitchen cupboard. When the bottle was empty, I would go down to the basement and fill it from a gallon jug of whiskey we stored there. When the gallon jug was empty, I would fill it up with a siphon hose from one of the 15-gallon barrels of whiskey we had in storage.

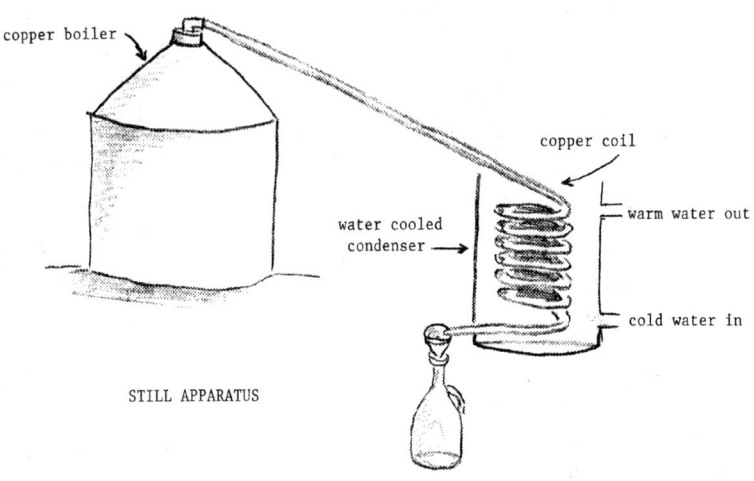

78. A drawing of our moonshine still.

The first time I siphoned moonshine as a youngster, I accidentally got some in my mouth (it tasted horrible) and I quickly spit it out. Even though moonshine was readily available to me, I rarely drank whiskey, even when I was older. When I had a toothache, I would take a small amount of moonshine in my mouth for a little while. The moonshine made the gum numb and also dulled the pain. After a while I spit out the moonshine; it left a sharp burning feeling in my mouth.

When relatives and friends visited us, we served them our moonshine. Sometimes paying customers would bring their own bottle to be filled. They were happy to be able to buy our moonshine because it was relatively cheap and convenient to purchase.

Joe Baldino told me that his father, who lived in Big Mine Run, made small quantities of moonshine for their own consumption. Some other families in the area also just made small amounts of moonshine.

Making larger quantities of moonshine, as we did, was much more dangerous. Revenue men were more interested in catching those making relatively large amounts of moonshine since they did not want people selling it.

A local politician would often warn us that some revenue men might be coming around to check on people suspected of making moonshine. When we received that information, we quickly stored all our moonshine apparatus in a pit in our basement floor that was not paved. Then we covered everything over with old boards and storage boxes.

After all, it was we against "them revenuers."

The *Shenandoah Evening Herald*, June 23, 1934:

WOMAN IS ARRESTED FOR OPERATING TWO STILLS

Mrs. Mary Zaggorsky, Mahanoy City, was committed to the county prison in default of $1,000 bail on charges of possession and operation of two liquor stills at her home, following a hearing before Squire M. F. Anderson, Mahanoy City.

Mrs. Zaggorsky was arrested when her home was raided by Investigator Marotte, special agent for the Pennsylvania Liquor Control Board. The raid followed a slight fire at the Zaggorsky home yesterday morning. Numerous complaints had been made by residents of the vicinity. Mahanoy City police joined in the raid.

The *Shenandoah Evening Herald*, Sept. 17, 1935:

FRACKVILLE COUPLE GUILTY OF DISTILLING

Court House, Pottsville. Sept. 17 – Albert and Helen Bubble, Frackville, were found guilty this morning of illegally manufacturing liquor in a jury verdict which recommended mercy.

The verdict was returned to Judge B. R. Jones, presiding in the Bruno trial. They had deliberated more than 12 hours since late yesterday, being locked up all night.

On charges of illegally possessing liquor, the couple was found not guilty and the jury split the costs between them and Louis Feldman, the prosecutor, an officer of the State Liquor Control board.

The Ashland Daily News, Oct. 30, 1935:

Drunken Driving Up 75% Since Repeal Was Put Over

Harrisburg. (UP) – Automobile accidents registered a 21 percent increase and arrests for drunken driving jumped 75% since repeal of the prohibition laws in Pennsylvania, according to W. W. Matthews, Chief of the Bureau of Safety, of the Department of Revenue.

The *Shenandoah Evening Herald*, July 30, 1936:

100-GALLON STILL TAKEN IN RAID AT GIRARDVILLE

Liquor control agents raided an apartment at 37 West Ogden Street, Girardville, and yesterday afternoon and arrested Theresa Bracale, after confiscating a 100-gallon still, 600 gallons of mash and 25 gallons of whiskey.

She was given a hearing today before United States Commissioner Reese at Tamaqua and then committed to jail in default of $100 state bail. The hearing was continued on another charge of violating the federal internal revenue laws and her bail will probably be fixed at an additional $2,500.

Commissioner Reese issued warrants for he arrest of Anthony Adormato ad Nicodemus Sozzloari, wanted in connection with the same case. A United States marshal will serve the warrants.

The *Shenandoah Evening Herald*, Nov. 18, 1937:

STILL EXPLODES AND SETS FIRE TO TUSCARORA HOME

Ms. Elizabeth Paytak, of Tuscarora, was arrested by Liquor Control board agents yesterday afternoon, after a still had exploded and set fire to the kitchen of her home.

The fire was discovered by an Orwigsburg State Motor Patrolman, who dashed into the house and rescued the woman after she was burned slightly about the face and hands.

The patrolman, after an investigation, discovered the cause of the fire and summoned the liquor agents. Mrs. Paytak will be charged with illegally maintaining a still.

The *Shenandoah Evening Herald*, Feb. 20, 1939:

RAID 150-GALLON STILL IN OLD BARN AT ASHLAND

Three agents of the State Liquor Control Board raided an old barn on South Third Street, Ashland, yesterday morning at 5 o'clock and apprehended five men operating a 150-gallon liquor still.

The agents, with the aid of an acetylene torch, burned a hole in the still and took some of the contents to be used as testimony against the five men. The contents were shipped by truck to Philadelphia.

The names of the men arrested were not disclosed. The barn was formerly used as a bootleg breaker.

FDR and Civil Rights

79. A woman with her child.

A number of New Deal programs did help African-Americans, even in the face of existing traditions of segregation. Roosevelt, however, was not a strong supporter of civil rights. Even early in his first administration in 1934, he did not strongly endorse an anti-lynching bill offered by several senators. Furthermore, he also refused to support anti-lynching bills, which were filibustered by southern Democrats in the Senate in 1937 and 1939.

Burton W. Folsom Jr. wrote, "For whatever reasons, Roosevelt was wary of forming close political ties with black Americans and he used no political capital to support civil rights during the New Deal years." On the other hand, a small number of New Dealers, including Eleanor Roosevelt were strongly supportive of civil rights.

80. Eleanor Roosevelt and Marian Anderson.

In 1939, the Daughters of the American Revolution (DAR) refused to let Marian Anderson perform in Constitution Hall in Washington, D.C. because of her race. As a result, Eleanor Roosevelt resigned her membership in the DAR. She then arranged for Ms. Anderson to give a performance at the Lincoln Memorial. There were 75,000 people in attendance.

81. Marian Anderson performing at Lincoln Memorial, 1939.

Finally, on June 13, 2005, the Senate formally apologized for its failure to enact anti-lynching bills. The resolution pointed out that 200 anti-lynching bills were introduced to Congress during the first half of the 20th century and the House of Representatives approved three. The Senate failed to pass any.

It is of interest to note that the Congress never passed an anti-lynching bill. Although lynchings were rare following the civil rights movement, they did occur.

The *Shenandoah Evening Herald*, May 16, 1936:

2 NEGROES BURNED TO DEATH BY CROWD; MURDERED BY SHERIFF

By L.S. Willis
United Press Staff Correspondent

Gordonville, Va., May 16. (U.P.) – Two negroes killed a sheriff, wounded five other white men, held off a posse numbering up to 5,000 men in a six-hour gun battle, and died, finally in a barrage of machine gun bullets in their blazing home early today.

Two hours later, after the ruins had cooled enough to permit approach, members of the posse raked the ashes and recovered one of the bodies. It was torn and cut up and parts of it, including some of the bones, were carried off as souvenirs.

The body of the second Negro – a woman – was recovered several hours later. It was dragged from the smoldering ruins and left for the curious to stare at and the few remaining souvenir hunters to dismember.

The battle raged under the glaring spotlights of fire trucks. Mountaineers from the surrounding Blue Ridge foothills with their traditional long barreled "shootin' arms," citizens with pistols and shotguns, state and local police with machine guns and automatic rifles were on one side and an elderly Negro man and his sister, armed with rifles and shotguns, were on the other.

At least 10,000 rounds of ammunition were expended. At times the barrage was so terrific it echoed and re-echoed over the hilltops and could be heard for miles.

The dead were Sheriff William Young of Orange County and the Negroes – William Walles, 60, and his sister, Cora, 62.

The *Shenandoah Evening Herald*, Aug. 14, 1936:

NEGRO KILLER HANGS AS CARNIVAL CROWD OF 15,000 WATCHES

Fran Leary
United Press Staff Correspondent

Owensboro, Ky., Aug. 14. (U.P.) – From a high gallows at dawn today, a Negro (murderer) looked down upon a carnival crowd of 15,000 spectators and an instant later dropped through the trap to eternity.

Mrs. Florence Thompson, the woman sheriff, had intended until the last minute to spring the trap on Rainey Bethea, 22, who raped and murdered a 70-year-old white woman. She lost her nerve and designated Harry Hasch, a former policeman.

While Bethea swung at the end of the rope, many in the crowd munched hot dogs and sipped soft drinks through straws. Vendors moving through the crowd shouting, "hot buttered pop corn–get your hot buttered pop corn; hot dogs–who wants a hot dog?" ceased their cries for the few minutes it took the huge negro to march up the gallows steps and die.

As the body dropped with a loud "pop" and the trussed body of the Negro plunged through, the crowd cheered and yelled.

Spectators had come by automobile, bus, train, and wagon from points as distant as Missouri, Indiana and Illinois.

Bethea dined on chicken and pork chops, ice cream, and watermelon. He demanded a second helping of one of the three desserts of his meal – lemon pie.

The Rev. John Thompson, Catholic priest, who had received his confession, followed him up the steps. The hangman paused to give him an opportunity to speak. He said nothing. The noose was adjusted and Hasch, immaculate in white linen and a white panama hat, pulled the lever. An instant before, Father Thompson patted his shoulder.

The *Shenandoah Evening Herald*, Feb. 2, 1937:

NEGRO IS LYNCHED BY ALABAMA MOB OF ONE HUNDRED

Abbeyville, Ala., Feb. 2. (U.P.) – Wesley Johnson, 22-year-old Negro, was taken from the county jail today and lynched by a mob of approximately 100 men.

Many members of the mob carried shotguns. They forced their way into the jail, covered Sheriff Louis Corbett and his jailer and seized the prisoner.

Bud Corbett, father of the sheriff and county jailer, said the Negro was held on a charge of attempting to assault Mrs. Rubert Barnes.

He was taken to the scene of the alleged attempted assault, hanged and riddled with bullets, the jailer explained.

The lynching was the first reported in Alabama in more than a year.

Governor Bibb Graves, after learning of the lynching, asked Attorney General A.A. Carmichael, to investigate impeachment proceedings against Sheriff Corbett.

He telephoned the sheriff and asked for an explanation. The sheriff gave the details of the lynching, the Governor said, but did not answer his question when asked, "Why did you keep it a secret so long?"

Playing Games

Many kids growing up during the 1930s were too young to grasp the full impact of those hard times. Life was simpler then; we had more free time compared to the many activities youngsters choose to become involved in today. We often made up our own games as well as our own rules.

It was always easy to start a baseball game. We only needed a sponge rubber ball, which we called a "spongy," and a wooden stick or paddle (we had no regular bat) to get the game started.

When we got a little older (around age 13 or 14) we would play with a hard ball we called a "tapey." We made the tapey by wrapping a golf ball in black tape until it was about the size of a regular baseball. By this time we had managed to get a regular baseball bat, but we rarely had more then one or two gloves. The person playing first base always got to use the first glove.

We played tag football because we always played on a hard dirt covered surface. Our football was a small empty milk can about the size of an ordinary can of soda. The can was often thrown hard and if you didn't catch it properly it would hit the tips of your fingers and really hurt.

On occasion some kid would get a regular football for a present. He immediately became popular because we all wanted to play with his football. And when the kid who owned the football had to go home, he always took his ball with him. We would, however, continue playing with our "can football."

I had a small hand-held cap pistol, which probably cost about 49 cents at the time. For a few pennies more, I could buy a small paper roll of red caps, which were used as "bullets" for the gun. I simply tore off one red paper dot and placed it in my pistol. When I pressed the trigger, the paper bullet went off with a "bang" along with a tiny puff of smoke. It was almost like the cowboy movies, which we were fond of watching.

Before I got my cap pistol, I would still go the candy store to buy a paper roll of red caps. I would tear off a single red cap from the roll and place it on the pavement. Then I took a small rock and struck the cap. The paper bullet went off with the same "bang" and smoke as it did when it went off in my pistol. It was more fun, however, shooting the cap pistol at another kid.

We also played with water pistols. The cheapest ones cost about 39 cents. In order to fill the pistol, you had to pull back on the trigger and then immerse the tip of the barrel of the gun in water. After releasing the trigger, a small amount of water was drawn up into the pistol. When you pointed your pistol at another kid and pressed the trigger, a short steady fine stream of water was ejected from the gun. He would duck under the water stream or run away. After that one shot, you had to reload your pistol and that took a little time. In the meantime, he would shoot his pistol at you.

Later, they made water pistols that held much more water. You could squirt stream after stream of water at another kid. And of course, he could do the same thing to you. We now felt more like our real cowboy heroes who could shoot their six shooters without reloading.

One of or most popular games was playing marbles. Every kid had his own small bag of marbles with a few knucklers in it. We used a multi-colored glass marble called a "knuckler" to shoot at a marble or at another kid's knuckler. In the process of shooting the glass-colored marble, we got down on one knee and with our hand on the ground we held our thumb over our bent forefinger and flicked off the knuckler with our thumb. Every mom knew that her little boy always wore out his jeans at the knees first from kneeling down on the ground to play marbles, and when she found a few marbles in one of his pockets, she knew that they were to be put aside to be given to her child to play another day.

I wheeled an old discarded automobile tire around for fun – other kids did the same thing. We would race each other, wheeling our tires as fast as we could run. We would bump our tires into each other's to try to knock them over. Can you imagine that being fun to do today?

We also played "kick the can." It was similar to baseball; however, the batter at home plate placed a partially crushed small can on the front of his shoe and then kicked the can as far as he could with a football-like kick. As the batter ran around the bases, the lone fielder would retrieve the can and touch home plate before the runner reached a base safely. The game required no ball, no gloves and no bat.

We played another game, which really had no name nor did it need one. We tramped down on a small can with one foot so that the sides of the can caved in and became attached to our shoe. We did the same thing with the other foot. Then several of us would go walking briskly about on the pavement with a crushed can on each foot, bumping into each other and making an awful racket. If a can happened to come loose, we would just reach down and tramp on it again and go on making more noise. On occasion, adults would suggest that we go somewhere else and make noise.

One of our favorite games was cops and robbers. It started with several players on each team. The kids on one team would hide in a number of different places, but in one general area. The other team would do the same thing. The idea was to not only find a secure place to hide, but to also be able to move around to another place without getting shot.

We didn't use any kind of toy guns. Whenever anyone recognized a person on the opposing team moving, he would call out, "Bang, bang, your dead," and follow up with the person's name or location. That player was then eliminated from the game. The game went on with each team trying to outshoot the other group. The last kid who did not get shot won the game for his team. The winner was generally that kid who could find a good place to hide as well as move about if necessary.

As I was writing this story, I received an e-mail from Fred Baldino, who now lives in California. In the 1930s, Fred grew up in Big Mine Run. He was several years older than me, but I knew him well. Airborne Fred was a paratrooper in World War II. He told me that the skills and techniques he learned from playing cops and robbers – hide-and-seek – as a kid in Big Mine Run saved his life several times while fighting the Germans in Europe.

The free time we had as youngsters may have allowed us the opportunity to be somewhat creative in our play. Arguably, the tactics and strategies we learned (along with risk-taking) when playing those made-up games with our own rules were valuable lessons that served us well later in life.

Guerney (Gike) Buhl

Guerney Buhl lived at four Woodland Heights; only five double dwelling houses down the street from our home. Guerney's nickname was "Gike" and that's what everyone called him. In the early fall of 1932, Gike was injured at the Bast Colliery in Big Mine Run. I was just 8 years old, but I remember it and also recall people talking about the accident.

Joanne Vaughn provided me with the following article on Gike's accident.

The Ashland Daily News, Aug. 22, 1932:

Miner Badly Hurt at Bast This Afternoon

Guerney Buhl, 24, of Woodland Heights, near Big Mine Run, was critically injured this afternoon when he was caught in a premature explosion of a charge of dynamite he had set inside the Bast mine of the Pennsylvania and Reading Coal and Iron Company.

The workman had his right hand blown off at the wrist. Three fingers of his left hand were so badly damaged that it was feared they would have to be amputated at the Ashland State Hospital.

Buhl was also suffering chest contusions and from extreme shock.

82. Gike was always busy.

Gike was transferred to the Wills Eye Hospital in Philadelphia. When he was finally discharged, we learned that he had lost his sight and also part of his right hand. His wife, Lillian, had four small children at the time – Betty, Ruth, Charles and Edward.

Gike was an amazing person, and I marveled at his upbeat nature. He adjusted to his tragic accident so well that he was an inspiration to others. He would crawl underneath his own automobile to repair it. He would simply ask for various wrenches and tools to get the job done. He was very clever and could do almost anything.

One summer afternoon my playmates and I were sitting around looking for something to do. Gike suggested that we play some athletic games that he played as a youngster. We were not familiar with any of the games he described; however, we found them to be simple, rough and fun games to play. Gike enjoyed listening to us play and talk about the games. We always went to him when we had a difference of opinion (an argument) about a particular ruling in a game he suggested – and he liked to play the role of referee. I'm sure it took him back to another time when he was just a kid playing those same games.

He was also very good at playing checkers. The checkerboard had cut outs where round and square pieces fit into their appropriate slots. He particularly enjoyed playing for a beer because he always won. I played several games of checkers with him and lost. He was always polite and wished me luck when I handed him a bottle of beer. He would say, "Here's to ya, 'Boya'," which was one of my nicknames.

One day Gike decided to show a group of young lads that he could tell the different values of paper money by gently rubbing his fingers over the numbers on the bill. When he was handed a bill, he would carefully rub his fingers over it and say, "This is a two dollar bill. This one is a five-spot. This one is a dollar bill." He always guessed correctly.

It turned out that he always performed this feat at a table where he had a confidant seated next to him. While Gike was feeling and rubbing the bill, his confidant would tap on Gike's shoe with his own foot the number that corresponded to the bill Gike was holding in his hand. He won many beers with that trick. Later when we found out how he did it, we all had a good laugh.

Gike was a good fastball pitcher on the local baseball team. After his accident, he was fond of listening to baseball games, especially the New York Yankees. Along with listening to shortwave radio, he would also listen to citizen band (CB) radio.

83. A bootleg mine accident near Shenandoah, Pa., 1936.

The last time I saw Gike was about 70 years ago, when I was still in high school. He was the most colorful and unforgettable character I knew in Big Mine Run. I never saw him in a depressed mood. While Gike may have lost his sight, he was a man who never lost his vision and love for life. He was 86-years-old when he died in 1995.

Miners Despair

The *Shenandoah Evening Herald*, Jan. 2, 1937:

MELANCHOLY MINER BLOWS SELF TO BITS

Presumably upset by melancholia induced by domestic troubles and drink, Enoch Gailushas, 46, seated himself on a discarded chair in a grimy shack at the rear of his home last night, hung a stick of dynamite around his neck and then calmly listened to the hissing of a burning fuse which discharged the explosive that blasted to bits his head and parts of his chest.

Neighbors, aroused by a strong powder smell, following a deafening explosion that rocked the neighborhood, led Police Officers Harry Kozar and John Toborowski to a small shanty, 40 feet in the rear of the dwelling, where the headless, bloody body was discovered slumped in the chair.

Deputy Coroner Francis Whalen arrived about 9:00 o'clock, an hour after the blast, and after close investigation termed the ghastly death a deliberate suicide.

Besides his wife and two daughters, there survives a son, Albert.

The *Shenandoah Evening Herald*, March 29, 1937:

MINER KILLS HIMSELF WITH DYNAMITE BLAST

Jacob Orbruzut, an unemployed miner about 55-years-old, committed suicide at 11:15 o'clock this morning by blasting his head off with a charge of dynamite in a small shanty at the rear of the home of Joseph Mickolajczyk, where he had been boarding.

Orbruzut, the family said, was single and had been living in the home for 21 years, never showing any signs of worry. Although unemployed for seven years and subsisting on direct relief and a meager income from coal "bootlegging," he was known as a jovial person until only recently when he menacingly mentioned dynamite. [Previously he had threatened to destroy himself with dynamite.]

He has no immediate survivors.

The *Shenandoah Evening Herald*, Oct. 16, 1937:

ARNOUT'S ADDITON MAN BLOWS HIMSELF TO DEATH

Alex Hrichak, 48-year-old miner, blew himself to death with dynamite at 10 o'clock this morning in the cellar of his home at Arnout's Addition, near St. Clair. He had steady employment at the St. Clair colliery and attributable motives could lot be learned. His widow and 10 children survive.

The *Shenandoah Evening Herald*, Nov. 11, 1937:

UNEMPLOYED MINER ENDS LIFE BY USING DYNAMITE

Peter Mercavage ended his life last night in the basement of his home at Tuscarora by discharging a stick of dynamite near his chest. State Motor Police of Tamaqua learned the man had been out of regular work about five years, but recently found work in a bootleg hole. His wife, two small daughters and one son were jarred by the explosion, which shook the house. Two married daughters in New Jersey also survive.

The *Shenandoah Evening Herald*, April 25, 1939:

MINER BLASTS SELF TO DEATH WITH DYNAMITE

Andrew Petruskey, Sr., 60, an unemployed miner, tied dynamite sticks around his neck this morning and blew himself into eternity.

Without disclosing his motive, he entered a front bedroom of his home, 520 East Centre Street, Shenandoah, just before noon and, within a few minutes an explosion shook the entire dwelling. His wife and daughter, downstairs, screamed with terror as the debris flew in all directions.

Petruskey's body was almost dismembered, parts being blown as far as the street. The detonation was so great that the four sides, ceiling and floor, of the bedroom were in splinters. The use of more than one stick of the charge was indicated by a huge gap in the wall between the front and middle bedrooms and the extensive damage to ceiling walls and furniture in the parlor directly below.

The family could offer no reason for the suicide. Neighbors thought highly of the man, explaining he had been a respected member of the community.

Deputy Coroner Francis Whalen, who arrived on the scene a few minutes after the explosion occurred, said, however, that ill health apparently was responsible. Petruskey, a former miner art Male Hill colliery, but unemployed the last seven hears, had a severe case of asthma, Whalen learned.

During questioning, Whalen was told that Petruskey went for a walk earlier in the morning. While returning he met his son Andrew, who was on his way to Maple Hill colliery to receive his pay.

Petruskey returned home, Whalen said, and asked his wife to press his trousers, while he went upstairs to rest.

Only a few more minutes elapsed when the tragedy occurred.

Petruskey, a member of St. George's Church, leaves his widow, Tessie, and the five following children: Andrew, Jr., at home; Michel,

Newark, N. J.; Mrs. Margaret Kilkuski, Shenandoah; Mrs. Anna Stancavage, Frackville, and Violet, at home.

Making Our Own Play Things

During the summer months I made a paper airplane from an ordinary sheet of tablet paper, and other kids did the same thing. We would compete with each other trying to make the airplane that would fly higher and longer than the next kid's. We tossed our "no-cost" paper airplanes for hours. They were great, because they would fly completely differently depending on how you folded them.

84. A paper airplane.

I also made canoe-shaped paper boats from tablet paper. I would add small stones in the boat for ballast and then place it in a creek that flowed past the schoolyard. The small boat would generally travel downstream some distance and I would run along side the creek following its progress. Sometimes older kids would throw stones at the paper boats to try to sink them.

We made our own "peashooters" from a hollow tubular plant, which was about the thickness of a ballpoint pen. The peashooters were about eight inches long and we blew small green wild cherries (our pellets) at one another. The peashooters were fragile and would break easily, but if they broke we would just make another one. If you happened to shoot pellets at an older kid, it was likely he would come over and take your peashooter and crush it. You would be lucky not to get a kick in the rear-end to boot.

We made an inner tube gun, which was made of wood and was about one foot long. The bullets were rubber bands made from a discarded automobile tire inner tube. The rubber bands or rings, looked like old-fashioned garters.

The wooden gun was constructed in such a manner that when you pressed the trigger, the rubber ring would be launched a reasonable distance. When you were struck at close range with a flying ring, it would really sting. We all carried extra rubber rings on our belt as we played, shooting at one another. We were trying to act like the cowboys who always had a belt with bullets when we saw them in the movies on a Saturday afternoon.

85. Using a slingshot.

I also made a slingshot, which I carried around in my back pocket. We generally shot small round stones at cans, bottles or similar objects. There were times, however, when we propelled stones at other kids. We were always a good distance apart so no harm was done. Nevertheless, it was a bad practice because a slingshot was still capable of propelling a stone with such force that it could seriously hurt someone.

Going to the Movies

The money I earned from picking huckleberries went for household expenses. When I went picking huckleberries the second time in one day, I was allowed to keep that money. I was also permitted to keep any money I earned by selling "old stuff" to the junkman when he came around.

My earnings allowed me to attend a Saturday matinee (where Tom Mix, Buck Jones, Bob Steele, Ken Maynard and other cowboys reigned). The Temple Theater, which showed those wonderful cowboys movies, was located at Sixth and Centre Street in Ashland.

Several of us would get together and walk to the theater, which was about one and one-half miles away. The price of admission was one dime. All of the kids from Big Mine Run always sat in the same place in the movie house.

The weekly serials were fun to watch. At the end of each episode, the hero or heroine would always be facing extreme danger and you were left with the impression that they would surely be killed. The following week, however, they always managed to miraculously escape. We would laugh and applaud our heroes. Each week we went through the same routine.

After the show we walked together talking about the movie all the way home. It was a wonderful way to spend a Saturday afternoon. Unknowingly, we were saying, "Depression, go away for a while."

The Depression Continues

86. Rural rehabilitation clients in Arkansas.

While the stock market picked up in the mid-1930s, it fell significantly later in the decade. The value of most stocks dropped in half from 1937 to 1939. The Depression was persistent. From November 1937 to August 1939, monthly unemployment ranged between 17 and 20 percent. During that time, approximately 9.5 million people were still out of work. Even as late as June 1939, federal works programs still supported almost 19 million people, nearly 15 percent of the country's population.

87. The Homer Shearer family in Estherville, Iowa.

The *Shenandoah Evening Herald*, June 27, 1936:

275 MINERS TO BE JOBLESS AS COMPANY CLOSES MINE

Two hundred and seventy-five employees at the Westwood colliery near Tremont and Tower City, will be thrown out of work Tuesday when the operators of the colliery, the Hazle Brook Coal

Company, will turn over the operation to the landowners who are the McGreery Estate of Philadelphia.

The workers were told to remove their tools yesterday.

Unable to sustain continued loss in operating, the necessity of going deeper to secure coal, and the impossibility of securing additional coal land on higher level, were given as the reasons for the coal company action.

A committee from the towns affected will meet Monday night to discuss ways and means of having the mine and breaker continue.

There were, however, some signs that the nation's economy might begin to turn around.

The *Shenandoah Evening Herald*, Aug. 5, 1938:

Survey Discloses Business Upswing In Almost Every Section Of The Nation But The Coal Region

Chicago, Aug. 5. (U.P.) – Business in general is optimistic about the immediate future and in almost every section of the country there has been an upswing, a survey by the United Press showed today.

Leaders reported that the downward spiral of the first six months of 1938 had leveled off and a distinct upturn was noticeable – although business generally is below 1937 levels.

From the textile towns of New England to the motion picture studios of Hollywood came reports "pretty good," "more encouraging," "promising," and "unusually favorable." The principal dark spot was in the coalfields of Pennsylvania.

Pennsylvania's State Secretary of Mines Michael J. Hartneady summed up the situation this way: "There is nothing bright in the near future for the Pennsylvania mining industry, except an early winter and cold as hell."

Hartneady said most of the companies are stocked to capacity with coal ready for market. He said none of the mines has been operating more than half time for the past four months, some not at all.

The *Shenandoah Evening Herald,* June 15, 1939:

ABANDON LYTLE COLLIERY 700 MINERS OUT OF WORK

Charles Grumm, superintendent of the Lytle Coal Company at Minersville, announced today that the Lytle colliery will be abandoned, throwing 700 miners into idleness.

The men were ordered to remove their tools and other equipment.

Bootleg mining and failure of the Legislature to pass the Kane Anthracite Bill were given as the causes by company officials.

The Lytle Coal Company is a subsidiary of the Susquehanna Collieries Company, former operators of the Wm. Penn colliery.

Superintendent Grumm formerly served in the same capacity at Wm. Penn colliery. He was transferred about two years ago when Tony Rose, Pittston independent operator, took over the mine.

The *Shenandoah Evening Herald,* Dec. 12, 1939:

$14 A MONTH FOR FAMILY OF 8

Mrs. Gertrude White finds it an almost hopeless task feeding her family of eight on Cleveland's reduced relief rations. Allowances, which once averaged $20 a month, have been reduced to approximately $14 monthly. She had three children: Edith 8, Gertrude, 1, and Phyllis, 5. (Central Press).

The *Shenandoah Evening Herald*, Jan. 18, 1940:

BANDITS KILL WATCHMAN TO OBTAIN $35.15

An intensive police hunt is under way for the bandits who brutally murdered a 63-year-old bootleg breaker watchman and then robbed him of $35.15 early this morning.

The body of Robert D. Evans, 612 Seneca Street, Pottsville, was found sprawled on the floor of a small office at the operation located near the Cotton Club on the old Pottsville-Schuylkill Haven highway.

Evan apparently was felled by vicious blows to the head and neck with a blunt instrument. An autopsy was to be performed this afternoon by Dr. W. R. Glenney, Pottsville.

The murder was discovered at 6:30 o'clock by William Gradwell, 16, of Cape Horn, who almost daily went to the breaker vicinity to pick coal, which had fallen from trucks.

The youth called for Evans as usual but there was no response. Then he peered through the window and saw the victim on the floor. He broke the front door down and, after failing to arouse Evans, summoned aid.

The attack occurred about 2 o'clock, police learned, and Evans apparently was struck suddenly, possibly during a conversation with the bandits. Police contended that Evans would have used his revolver if he suspected the robbery.

Pockets of Evan's clothes were turned out, indicting that he was robbed after he collapsed from the blow. Police said the bandits took a small bag containing $25.15 from Evan's pockets and scooped the other $10 from the desk drawer.

88. A ten-year-old cotton picker fixing the family car.

In 1934, FDR appointed Henry Morgenthau Jr. as Secretary of the Treasury. Morgenthau served in that position until 1945. It is of interest to note that he believed in balancing the budget, lowering the national debt and favoring more investment by the private sector. After serving FDR for a number of years, he concluded that the New Deal programs did not end the Depression. According to Burton Folsom Jr., Morgenthau made the following surprising statement to the House Ways and Means Committee in May 1939.

> We have tried spending money. We are spending more than we have ever spent before and it does not work. And I have just one interest, and if I am wrong ... somebody else can have my job. I want to see this country prosperous. I want to see people get a job. I want to see people get enough to eat. We have never made good our promises... . I say after eight years of this Administration we have just as much unemployment as when we started .... And an enormous debt to boot!

It is surprising that many daily newspapers, including the *Shenandoah Evening Herald*, which cost two cents in 1929, did not increase to three cents until January 1938. It was an indication of how scarce money was eight years after the stock market crashed.

The *Shenandoah Evening Herald*, Jan. 15, 1938:

HERALD SUBSCRIPTION PRICES ADVANCE JAN. 17

Unable to offset the rapidly advancing cost of production, paper, taxes, newsprint, extra demands upon service to the public and the constant expanding requirements for news coverage, all regional newspapers commencing Monday morning will sell for three cents a single copy.

Besides the *Evening Herald*, other papers to increase their subscription fees are the *Pottsville Journal*, *Pottsville Republican*, *Tamaqua Evening Courier*, *Ashland Daily News*, *Mahanoy City Record-American*, *Mt. Carmel Item*, *Hazleton Plain Speaker*, *Hazleton Standard-Sentinel*, and *Shamokin News-Dispatch*.

The increase prices are in line with prices charged by the vast majority of daily newspapers throughout the United States.

Sledding Downhill

>Childhood is such a short season.
>–Helen Hayes

Sledding was the most enjoyable thing I did outdoors during the winter. I started from the top of the hill at Woodland Heights and traveled down a steep slope for about 100 yards to Big Mine Run. Most of the time I would go sledding "belly bumper" style (lying flat on my stomach on the sled as I went downhill). When I got to the bottom I would pull my sled back up the hill and do it again. Kids who didn't have a sled could usually get a ride down the hill with somebody else. On the way downhill it was common to see kids throw snowballs at others sledding by.

89. Wally Baran sledding, age 11.

There were times when I went so fast (the hill was quite steep) that my eyes teared up so badly I could hardly see. When that happened, I had to veer off the road and run into a snow bank to slow down and eventually stop. The hill that we sledded down was the same road the automobiles used and it was only wide enough for one car at a time. If we saw a car coming uphill as we were going down, we had to quickly turn off to one side to get out of the way.

After sledding for hours, I would slowly start walk home pulling my sled along. As I got closer to my home, I was thinking about how nice it would be to get something good to eat. When I got home, I would take off my hat, coat and shoes. Then I would sit on a chair and open the oven door on the coal stove and place my feet at the edge of the oven door to get warm. As I was getting nice and warm my Mom would hand me a snack – a jelly sandwich, which tasted great.

The Circus Is in Town

I often visited the circus grounds when the caravan of trucks, wagons and circus people arrived in Ashland. I enjoyed watching the men putting up the big tent. One time I carried water in a bucket for the elephants to drink and earned a free pass for admission to the big tent. Frankly, I would have carried the water for nothing just to see the elephants up close and sometimes even touch their trunks.

The big attraction at the circus was the "Big Top." It was the place where all the action took place. It featured clowns, acrobats (including trapeze acts) and trained animals (elephants, lions, tigers, ponies and dogs).

My parents never went to the circus, so I just walked by myself to Ashland when the circus came to town. I rarely had a free pass, so I would peek under the big tent to see what was going on. The circus had their own security guard on the inside watching for kids who would try to "sneak in" under the big tent. Sometimes a guard would allow me to watch for a few minutes and then politely tell me to move on. I wonder if he may have thought about the time when he, too, was just a youngster.

One day I recall Mom telling me that when the circus came to town, many of the breaker kids would skip work and go to see the circus. The breaker kids were just that – they were young boys from the age of 10 to14 who were full-time employees in the coal breakers. The breaker kids not only worked long hours in poor working conditions, but their work was also hazardous. Those young boys were telling us in a poignant way that it is the right of a child to have a childhood.

Going to the Carnival

We all looked forward to the time when the carnival came to town. The carnival, which came once a year and stayed for a week, visited Girardville, two miles east of Big Mine Run. It was a traveling amusement show that was very popular and attracted large crowds of people.

There were a variety of games that people played trying to win attractive prizes as well money; however, the games were designed (better, rigged) so the customer rarely won. When someone did win, it was generally a minor prize; nevertheless, people did try their luck and play those games.

The carnival also operated a variety of rides that were particularly popular with kids. It was fun for us to watch the merry-go-round with the loud music, and the huge Ferris Wheel always attracted a lot of attention.

I would just walk around with other kids from Big Mine Run looking at everything that was free. One popular event was called the side show. Performers would come out from a tent onto a temporary stage and put on a short free show. The barker would talk loud and fast describing how much more you would see on the inside of the tent. After the free show, the barker would say, "Yes ladies and gentlemen, all that and much more for just one thin dime."

One side show always featured scantly clad dancing girls. When we looked at them, we would gently bump each other, as young kids tend to do meaning, "look at that."

Another sideshow would bring out fire-eaters and sword swallowers. Other shows would feature grotesque figures like the tattooed lady, the world's strongest man, the snake man, the smallest person in the world and the tallest man in the world. Even though the barker always exaggerated what you would see on the inside of the tent, people didn't seem to mind too much if they were fooled a little.

The carnival was not only entertaining but something different from our ordinary lives and everyone seemed to have a good time. About 11 p.m., several of us kids would start our two-mile walk back home to Big Mine Run, talking about all the things we saw and dreaming about what it would be like to be a member of a traveling carnival show.

Playing Cards

Our family frequently played card games, especially during the winter months when we spent a lot of time indoors. Our entire family played cards; it was one of the most enjoyable things we did.

Pinochle was popular, where two partners played two others. There were other variations of pinochle that we also played. Hearts was another game we liked to play, where the terrible queen of spades was to be avoided if you wanted to win. We also played other games like old maid, poker, rummy, solitaire, black jack, war, and steal the pile.

Life was simpler during those depression years, especially if you lived in a patch town like Big Mine Run. Just think, an ordinary deck of playing cards kept us entertained all winter long. In a way it also kept our entire family together.

The Old Swimming Hole

We had a favorite swimming hole that was situated in a wooded, isolated area about one half of one mile from Big Mine Run. It was a natural spring-fed pond. The water was always cold had a blue-green color so we called it "the Bluey."

Whenever we felt like going for a swim on a hot summer day, several of us would hike to the Bluey; sometimes we would go swimming twice if it was hot enough.

When we arrived at the Bluey, we generally started a small wood fire so that we could get warm after coming out of the pool. Of course, we all went swimming naked – nobody had a swimsuit.

Huckleberries grew in the area and it wasn't unusual to hear berry pickers calling to each another while we were standing around the fire and chatting. On occasion someone would holler out, "some girls are coming toward the pool!" All of a sudden four or five naked boys would make a dash for the pool. It always turned out to be a false alarm, and we would laugh about it afterward.

We always wanted to see who was courageous enough to go for the first swim early in the spring when the water was unusually cold. Whenever that happened, the word soon spread and then we all knew who took the first swim. It turned out that it was usually an older person and it was considered to a "big deal." More importantly, it was an early sign that before too long we all would be headed up to the Bluey for our first swim of the year.

The Early 1940s

Bootlegging Coal Still Going Strong

The *Shenandoah Evening Herald*, Dec. 15, 1939:

Bootleg Holes Are Increasing Survey Reveals

A survey of bootleg mine operations being conducted by the State Department of Mines has disclosed that there are more illegitimate mines in this area than ever before.

James Quigley, state mine inspector for the 23rd district, last night told newspapermen at Mt. Carmel, that he personally visited 89 bootleg holes yesterday. Mr. Quigley's disclosure came as a surprise as the general impression was that bootleg mines were on the decline, not because of a reduction in unemployment but rather a scarcity of suitable sites to drive holes.

Mr. Quigley declared that the various coal holes produced an average of from two to 20 tons of coal per day and employed an average of four men per bootleg mine.

He estimated that about one-half of the population in the lower anthracite field depended on the bootleg mines for a livelihood.

The *Shenandoah Evening Herald*, July 26, 1940:

TWO MEN KILLED IN BOOTLEG MINE MISHAP

Two Phoenix Park men were killed this morning when gearing on a make-shift mine "buggy" broke, plunging them down a 300-foot mine slope.

The victims were William Switzer, Sr., 57, and his son-in-law, Philip E. Purcell, 37. Both died instantly of multiple fractures. Switzer's son, William, 25, the third person on the mine car, is in the Pottsville Hospital with fractured vertebrae and multiple contusions of the body and legs. His condition is "fair."

The three men were descending the slope at 7:30 o'clock when suddenly the cable snapped, causing the "buggy" to roll down the 70-degree grade at a terrific speed. The elder Switzer and Purcell were thrown out by the jar and mangled by the car as it sped down.

The son, however, who was sitting in the middle, remained on the car until it hit the bottom. The impact threw him out, but he managed to crawl up the tracks of the slope and reach the surface 15 minutes later.

The bodies of Switzer and his son-in-law were not recovered until a half-hour later. Volunteer rescuers removed the fallen cable and cautiously tested the sides and ceiling of the slope as they descended for the bodies.

John Lynch, 20, also of Phoenix Park, was operating the automobile motor, which generated power for the hoist. He said the engine was in reverse when suddenly he heard the gears "click" and saw the cable separate. He called for help.

The elder Switzer leaves his widow and six children, while Purcell is survived by his widow and two children.

The *Shenandoah Evening Herald*, Aug. 5, 1940:

48th BOOTLEG FATALITY IS REGISTERED TO TODAY

The bootleg coal mining death toll in the Northumberland-Schuylkill County area since

January 1 rose to 48 today with the death of Andrew Dombroskie, 50, Shamokin.

Dombroskie was crushed beneath a fall of rock and dirt. Ben Sosnoskie, who was with Dombroskie when the fall occurred, also was trapped but managed to work himself free. He escaped with minor injuries.

Hilbert Kroh's Story

As a young lad, Hilbert Kroh lived just a very short distance down the road from our home in Woodland Heights. Even though he was two years older than I was, we often played outdoor games together.

Hilbert, along with other young lads in Big Mine Run, quit attending school to work in a coal hole. His death, along with many other bootleg miners, was a grim reminder of how dangerous it was to work in any coal hole.

I knew all five men who worked with Hilbert in that independent coal mine as well as all members of the immediate Kroh family.

Joanne Vaughn, from Ashland, provided me with the following article on Hilbert's death.

The Ashland Daily News, Dec. 18, 1941:

Mowry Youth Is Victim Bootleg Mine Accident

Nineteen-year old Hilbert Kroh, Mowry, was fatally injured yesterday afternoon at 1:30 o'clock when he was struck by a runaway "buggy" inside a bootleg coal mine between Homesville and Big Mine Run.

The youth was struck by the mine car after it plunged 100 feet down the mine slope. He suffered a fractured right jaw, a crushed face and from shock. He died at 6:40 o'clock last evening at the Ashland State Hospital where he was admitted at 2:20 p.m.

Young Kroh worked in the independent coal mine along with four of his brothers, Ralph of Big Mine Run, Roy and Arthur of Ashland, William of Mowry and Steven Hendricks, of Girardville.

He was sitting at the bottom of the slope when the accident occurred. The buggy had been hoisted to the surface and was braced on the tipple while a change was being made in the hoisting motor. A "laggin" [section of lumber] used to hold the mine car is reported to have snapped, releasing the heavy car and permitting it to run wild down the slope.

Kroh was driven 15 feet along the bottom by the impact and his brother, Ralph, working about 25 feet away, was attracted by the crash. He summoned another brother, Roy, also working inside at the time, and they lifted the car beneath which Hilbert was pinned.

The "buggy" was placed on the rails and the injured youth hoisted to the surface. He was unconscious when his brothers released him from beneath the car and died without regaining consciousness.

To survive besides his mother and the four brothers who worked with him in the coal mine are his stepfather, Ferdinand Enders, another brother, Albert at home, these sisters, Mrs. Gertrude Krah, Mrs. Eva Betrusky [Petrusky], Mrs. Lillian Buehl, all of Ashland, Mrs. Dorothy Cooney, St. Louis, MO, and Miss Evelyn, at home.

War In Europe

On Sept. 1, 1939, the German Army invaded Poland. Two days later both Great Britain and France declared war on Germany – it was the beginning of World War II.

FDR turned again to radio and in typical fashion tried to inform and comfort the public regarding the war in Europe. His fireside chat focused on the threat of war to America and not on the economy. He said, "I hope the United States will keep out of this war. I believe that it will, and I give you my assurance and reassurance that every effort of your government will be directed to that end."

By the end of the year, however, the threat of war would increasingly begin to receive more attention from FDR and Congress.

Government Spending Continues

In 1933, the federal government spent $4.5 billion and by 1940 that number had increased to about $9.4 billion. During that time, federal spending more than doubled and the national debt grew more than it had in the previous 150 years. In January 1940, unemployment remained stubbornly high at 14.6 percent; about eight million people were out of work. The Depression continued for eight years after Roosevelt was elected to his first term in 1932.

The *Shenandoah Evening Herald*, Jan. 5, 1939:

ROOSEVELT'S 1940 BUDGET AMOUNTS TO $9 BILLION SEEKS FUNDS FOR W.P.A. JOBS

Washington, D.C., Jan. 5. (U.P.) – President Roosevelt today asked Congress for an immediate $875,000,000 appropriation to provide W. P. A. jobs for between 3,000,000 and 2,700,000 persons until June 30, the end of the 1939 fiscal year.

He asked for these funds in a special relief message, while in his regular budget message, also submitted today, he projected a relief and recovery program of $2,266,165,000 for the new fiscal year beginning in July.

Our Family Situation Improving

It was June 1940 and I had just completed my sophomore year in high school. Finally, after 10 years, our family financial situation was improving. We went from being dirt poor to comfortably poor. By now, my two older sisters had been employed for several years and my youngest sister would soon also be employed. Mom continued to do housecleaning and laundry for three families.

While we were better of than a few years ago, there were times when I still wore second-hand shoes while attending high school, and my Uncle Bill and Aunt Mary usually paid for a new sweater or jacket when I needed one.

FDR's Third Term

The *Shenandoah Evening Herald*, Jan. 4, 1940:

F.D.R. 'Way Off' In Estimates Of Income, Expenses

Washington, Jan. 4, (U.P.) – In his five full fiscal years, President Roosevelt has underestimated New Deal spending by $6 billion and overestimated income by approximately $1.7 billion, analysis disclosed today.

Unexpected economic reverses and unforeseen conditions affecting agriculture were largely responsible for the discrepancies between the estimates and the final results.

Although the budget-makers appeared to have gone wide of their mark in forecasting spending, they erred only slightly in estimating income during the fiscal years 1935 to 1939 inclusive.

The *Shenandoah Evening Herald*, Aug. 1940:

More Taxes Asked Because Of $5.7 Billion Deficit

By John R. Beal

Washington, Aug. 8. (UP) – Secretary of the Treasury Henry Morgenthau, Jr., today forecast a record peace time deficit of approximately $5.7 billion and urged Congress to increase government revenue by enacting immediately an excess profits tax.

Morgenthau was the first witness before the House Ways and Means Committee in a general hearing on excess profits taxation. Less than two months ago Congress enacted a special tax bill increasing hundreds of nuisance, income, inheritance, and other levies to finance the gigantic rearmament program. Thee are several bills pending in Congress for drastic taxation of excess profits made on government orders.

Estimating receipts for the current fiscal year at $6.367 billion, the secretary predicted that total expenditures probably would exceed $12 billion.

The Selective Training and Service Act of 1940 (also known as the draft) was signed by FDR in September 1940. It required men between the ages of 21 and 30 to register with their local draft boards. One month later, men were being drafted for military service. It was the first peacetime conscription in the nation's history. It was the beginning of a drastic change in the United States when untold numbers of young men and women would shortly leave civilian life to serve in the military.

The *Shenandoah Evening Herald*, Oct. 2, 1940:

ORDER SCHOOLS CLOSED OCT. 16 TO SPEED DRAFT

Harrisburg, Oct. 2 (UP) – Governor Arthur H. James issued a proclamation today requesting officials of all Pennsylvania schools to declare October 16 a holiday to facilitate registration of the state's estimated 1.5 million prospective conscripts aged 21 through 35.

It was anticipated the State Liquor Control Board would also follow the proclamation with an order closing the 579 state liquor stores the entire registration day and directing the taprooms not to serve customers during the recording hours 7 a. m. to 9 p. m.

"Dismissal of approximately 2 million state school pupils October 16 will serve as a most effective reminder of the duty of all concerned and will make available school houses and buildings as places of registration," the proclamation said.

A formal request for such a proclamation was filed with James today by the Allegheny County commissioners. Philadelphia school authorities have already declared "R-Day" a holiday and requested teachers to assist without pay as registrars.

By 1940, FDR had assembled a very strong political machine. People generally not only liked Roosevelt, but they had confidence in him. Even "tough reporters" were overwhelmed by his charming personality.

Wendell Willkie, a corporate lawyer, was FDR's opponent in the upcoming election. Willkie was a much less experienced campaigner and was no match for Roosevelt.

Adam Cohen wrote, "In the 1940 election, Willkie made [Frances] Perkins an issue. He would appoint a secretary of labor from the labor movement, he promised a union crowd in Pittsburgh, adding, 'and it won't be a woman, either.'"

In November 1940, FDR was elected to an unprecedented third term. He defeated Willkie by a 449-82 electoral vote.

The *Shenandoah Evening Herald,* Nov. 6, 1940:

ROOSEVELT WINS THIRD TERM PRESIDENT TAKES SCHUYLKILL COUNTY

America Goes to War

On May 27, 1941, FDR declared an unlimited national emergency; we were moving with more urgency to prepare for a possible war. One month later, June 22, 1941, Germany invaded the Soviet Union. On Dec. 7, 1941, the Japanese attacked the United States fleet at Pearl Harbor – the world was at war. America's isolationism vanished overnight.

Federal spending increased drastically as millions of young men and women went to war. Furthermore, millions (especially women) also went off to work in factories manufacturing material for war. The increasing demand for war material drove unemployment below 10 percent in 1941. It was the first time unemployment was in single digits since 1929. The number of those without a job dropped to 5.3 million, only one-third of what it was when FDR took office.

In June 1942, I graduated from high school and went to work for the Sun Shipbuilding and Drydock Company in Chester, Pa. Jobs were available for almost anyone who wanted to work; unemployment was no longer a major problem for the country. The long economic nightmare for America was over.

After working for six months, I volunteered to serve in the United States Army.

Then and Now

It is clear that many people have suffered large financial losses during the present recession. The average person today, however, is not experiencing the same despair and hopelessness that the ordinary person did during the Great Depression.

Unemployment in September 1931 was 17.4 percent. It then went to an all-time high of 25% when FDR took office in early 1933. It never reached single digits until 1941. As the Great Depression went on and on, people were beginning to think they would live in squalor for the rest of their lives. That 10-year period was the most severe economic downturn in our nation's history.

In May 2009 unemployment was 9.4 percent and analysts predict it will reach 10 percent before we begin to have an economic recovery. While we are not certain when the present recession will end, no one believes that we will have to endure a decade of "hard times" like that of the Great Depression.

Finally, if you think the present recession is bad, take a hard look at photos of the Great Depression.

FDR's Legacy

FDR had to deal with the Great Depression, which was the worst economic downturn in American history. It was a complex worldwide crisis that was very difficult to handle.

Most historians agree that America's entry into World War II was the critical turning point in finally ending the Depression. A number of FDR's policies, which were started with high expectations that they would reduce unemployment and produce a strong economy, did not succeed.

Roosevelt and his New Deal policies did, however, change America significantly, and many of his basic principles are still with us today. He was the most dominating figure of his time in the United States. People felt that he was their friend and that he cared about them. They viewed his presidency as a "humane administration."

It would have been interesting to talk to FDR late in his presidency to get his views on what he would have done differently if he only had the chance to do it over again.

Scholars, however, are still researching other factors that also played an important role in ending the Depression. Some economists point out that FDR was unfriendly to businesses and raised corporate, income and excise taxes during the 1930s, which actually prolonged the Great Depression.

Roosevelt has been one of the most influential presidents in our history. Arguably, he is considered by many historians to be in the top three greatest presidents of all-time. Like Washington and Lincoln, FDR also served our nation in a time of peril and crisis.

President Obama's Administration

The Obama administration is moving toward larger and larger governmental intervention, control and power – even more than FDR did. The huge debt that we are incurring will be extraordinarily difficult to deal with in the future. If the Obama presidency continues to move in the direction as it has in the first 100 days, he could be changing America in a fundamental way.

George Santayana said, "Those who do not remember the past are condemned to repeat it." It would be unfortunate if present policy makers repeat the mistakes of previous administrations. Even though we do pay attention to the past, Mark Twain reminds us that, "History doesn't repeat itself, but it does rhyme."

APPENDIX

SOME HIGHLIGHTS OF THE WPA

(A (Very) Partial List by State

ALABAMA

Birmingham: Vulcan Park observation tower
Brundidge: "We Piddle Around" Theater (formerly Brundidge City hall)
Sylacauga: Isabel Anderson Comer Museum and Arts Center (formerly B.B. Comer Memorial Library)

ALASKA

Ketchikan: Federal Building

ARIZONA

Coolidge: Casa Grande Ruins National Monument
Naco: Turquoise Valley Golf Course club house

ARKANSAS

Jasper: Newton County Courthouse
Mountain Home: Baxter County Courthouse

CALIFORNIA

Clayton: Summit Building at Mount Diablo State Park
Mendocino County: Mendocino Woodlands State Park
San Bernardino County: Asistencia, Mission San Gabriel

San Francisco: Cow Palace, murals at Beach Chalet
San Jose: National Guard Armory

COLORADO

Denver: Bonnie Brae Park
Mesa Verde National Park: historic dioramas
Pueblo: City Park (including Lake Joy, Monkey Mountain, and Monkey Island), Pueblo Junior College

CONNECTICUT

New Haven: Chatfield Hollow State Park tower
Norwalk: Oak Hills Park Golf Course; murals at Norwalk City Hall, Norwalk Transit District, Norwalk Community College, Norwalk Public Library, and the Maritime Aquarium at Norwalk
Stamford: Michael A. Boyle Stadium

DELAWARE

Hancock: Hancock Golf Course

DISTRICT OF COLUMBIA

Washington: murals at Smithsonian American Art Museum

FLORIDA

Tavernier Keys: Monroe County Health Department (built as a school and hurricane refuge)
Fort Meyers: Fort Meyers Yacht Basin

GEORGIA

Clayton: nine-hole golf course at Rabun County Golf Club
Macon: Macon City Hall, Ocmulgee National Monument

HAWAII

Oahu and outer islands: civilian and military airfields

IDAHO

Arco: Recreation Hall
Boise: Ada County Courthouse and murals
Idaho Falls: Idaho Falls Airport Historic District

ILLINOIS

Aurora: Phillips Park Golf Course
Brookfield: Brookfield Zoo
Chicago: Zoo Rookery at Lincoln Park Zoo
Dixon: park system bridges and landscaping
Murphysboro: Riverside Park baseball field and band shell

INDIANA

Hammond: Hammond Civic Center
Michigan City: Washington Park Zoo improvements
Mishawaka: Battell Park band shell and rock garden

IOWA

Clinton: Stone Lookout Tower
Dubuque: Eagle Point Park, Shot Tower restoration

KANSAS

Hiawatha: National Guard Armory
Hutchinson: Prairie Dunes Golf Course

KENTUCKY

Ashland: Central Park, Putnam Stadium at Paul Blazer High School

LOUISIANA

Baton Rouge: Louisiana State University's Tiger Stadium
New Orleans: Crescent City Golf Course

MAINE

Caribou: Nylander Museum
Portland: Portland Observatory Maritime Signal tower restoration

MARYLAND

Cumberland: Constitution Park pool
Frederick County: Camp David presidential retreat

MASSACHUSETTS

Danvers: murals at Danvers Town Hall
Haverhill: Haverhill Stadium
Hyde Park: George Wright Golf Course
Melrose: Stone wall in Wyoming Cemetery
New Bedford: New Bedford Municipal Golf Course

MICHIGAN

East Lansing: East Wing and murals at Michigan State University's Kresge Art Museum
Kalamazoo: Milham Park Municipal Golf Course

MINNESOTA

Currie: Beach House and Mess Hall at Lake Shetek State Park

Roseau: Roseau City Hall

St. Paul: Keller Golf Course, Minnehaha Playground building

MISSISSIPPI

Carrollton: Carrollton Community House

Jackson: terminal building at Hawkins Field (airport), castle and Elephant House Café at Jackson Zoo

MISSOURI

Arrow Rock: open shelter and stone bridge at arrow Rock State Historic Site

St. Louis: picnic shelters at Tilles Park, Grand Staircase at Fort Belle Fontaine Park

MONTANA

Bozeman: Longfellow School

Kalispell: Buffalo Hill Golf Course

Lewistown: Rock ponds and bridges at Big Springs Trout Hatchery

Miles City: Denton Field baseball stadium

NEBRASKA

Lincoln: "The Smoke signal" sculpture at Pioneer Park

Nebraska City: Stone footbridge at Steinhart Park

NEVADA

Reno: Washoe County Golf Course, Southside School annex

NEW HAMPSHIRE

Laconia: Gunstock Mountain Lodge
Manchester: airport terminal building
Nashua: Holman Stadium

NEW JERSEY

Alpine: Lookout Inn on the Palisades Parkway
Newark: murals at Newark City Hall
Somerset: Great Swamp drainage ditches

NEW MEXICO

Claunch: Old School House
Fort Summer: mural at De Baca County Courthouse
Magdalena: old WPA gym

NEW YORK

Bethpage: Bethpage State Park golf course
Buffalo: Buffalo Memorial Auditorium
Bronx: Split Rock Golf Course
Fair Haven: Fair Haven Beach State Park
New York City: La Guardia Airport
West Point: stained glass and painted murals at U.S. Military Academy's Washington Hall (cadet mess)

NORTH CAROLINA

Cullowhee: Western Carolina University's Breese Gymnasium
Goldsboro: Old Station 1 fire station
Roanoke Island: Fort Raleigh National Historic Site

NORTH DAKOTA

Bismarck: Edwards House at Camp Grafton (North Dakota National Guard)
Linton: Emmons County Courthouse
Minot: Pioneer Bowl

OHIO

Akron: Rubber Bowl stadium at University of Akron
Cleveland: Forest Hill Park
Columbus: Ohio State University Golf Course

OKLAHOMA

Fort Gibson: Fort Gibson Historic Site restoration

OREGON

Eugene: Civic Stadium, Howe Memorial Gates at University of Oregon
Mount Hood: Timberline Lodge
Portland: Stone House at Forest Park

PENNSYLVANIA

Pittsburgh: Stone stairs and bridges at Schenley Park
Philadelphia: reading room at the Philadelphia Museum of Art Library buildings at Fairmount Park
York: WPA Models and Dioramas at Indian Steps Museum

RHODE ISLAND

Barrington: Stone fireplaces at Dr. George B. Haines Memorial Park
Providence: Stone staircase at Neutaconkanut Hill Park

SOUTH CAROLINA

Charleston: Dock Street Theatre restoration
Columbia: Mckissick Museum at University of South Carolina

SOUTH DAKIOTA

Philip: Philip Auditorium
Rapid City: Dinosaur Park

TENNESSEE

Bristol: Stone Castle Stadium at Tennessee High School
Kingsport, Johnson City, and Bristol tri-cities: airports in Memphis, Chattanooga, Knoxville, Nashville, and Jackson
Memphis: Children's Museum of Memphis (formerly National Guard Armory)
Nashville: Fort Negley restoration

TEXAS

Dallas: Dealey Plaza
La Porte: San Jacinnto Monument
San Antonio: River Walk

UTAH

Garfield County: Bryce Canyon Airport, between Escalante and Panguitch
Helper: Helper Civic Auditorium
Salt Lake City: rotunda murals at the Utah State Capitol

VERMONT

Montpelier: Recreation Park

VIRGINIA

Fredericksburg: Spotsylvania County Courthouse annex

WASHINGTON

Seattle: Woodland Park Zoo

WEST VIRGINIA

Fairmount: Stone walls at East-West Stadium

WISCONSIN

Hales Corner: Golf club house at Whitnall Park
Milwaukee: Sculptures at Parklawn Housing Project
Milwaukee County: swimming pools, pavilions, Milwaukee County park system

WYOMING

Casper: Natrona County High School
Dayton: Dayton Community Hall
Newcastle: Anna Miller Museum (building originally constructed for the Wyoming National Guard)

ACKNOWLEDGMENTS

Most of all, I would like to express a special thank you to my wife, Gloria, who has been my inspiration for writing this book. I am also grateful to the other members of our family: Chris, Karen, Greg, Arlene and Hattie for their encouragement and support.

I am especially grateful to Henry H. Nyce, publisher of *The Republican-Herald, The News-Item* and *The Citizen-Standard* who gave me permission to use articles from the *Shenandoah Evening Herald* and *The Ashland Daily News.* This book could not have been written without his gracious consent.

My editor, L. Reidar Jensen formerly the managing editor of the *Shippensburg News-Chronicle*, was a joy to work with. I owe him a special debt of gratitude for the superb job he did editing the manuscript and finding more errors than I care to think about. Reidar also provided valuable insights during our breakfast meetings to discuss all aspects of the book.

I want to thank Abbie Jensen for her helpful contributions. I was especially pleased to receive her excellent suggestions concerning the photos in the manuscript.

My sincere thanks to Rick "ranger" Kerr, Lt. Colonel U. S. Army (retired) for inserting all the photographs into the text. When I have a computer problem, I just call the Ranger Rick, who is my neighbor, and he solves the problem.

I have enjoyed my weekly coffee meetings with Dr. William Smith, my former colleague at Shippensburg University. Our conversations generally dealt with some aspect of the Great Depression.

Whenever I had some matter pertaining to photography, I always called upon Nick Kalathas, my friend, who is an expert photographer. He designed the front cover of the book and also took the photo on the back cover of the book. His superb website is www.naturesmoments.com.

A special thank you to Diane Kalthas and Teresa Strayer at the Shippensburg University Library for their assistance in obtaining books, and microfilm from their excellent Interlibrary Loan Department.

I want to thank Susan Hockenberry, Mary Mowery and Denise Wietry in the Circulation Department at Shippensburg University for their assistance on various matters.

I also want to acknowledge the help I have received from the following at the Shippensburg University: Dr. Douglas Cook, Karen Daniel, Aaron Dobbs, Dr. Signe Kelker and Kirk Moll.

My thanks to Wally Baran for providing photos and other information I requested from him. He was always gracious and ready to help.

I want to express my thanks to Wanda Kehler Edelman, my classmate at Butler Township High School, for the conversations we had about the Depression.

Joanne Vaughan has been helpful in locating several stories from *The Ashland Daily* News for me.

My sincere thanks to Dr. Diane Spokus for her encouragement and support. Diane is a faculty member in the Health Policy and Administration Department at The Pennsylvania State University. Her excellent website is http://www.personal.psu.edu/dms201/blogs/spokus/.

I was pleased to receive stories from Fred and Joe Baldino, two Big Mine Run lads, who I knew growing up during the Depression.

I want to thank the Shippensburg Historical Society for giving me permission to use the Peerless Furniture Company letter. My thanks also to Trisha Grace for scanning the document to me.

My thanks to Patty Flemister, Sandy Bryan and Jennifer Bryan for giving me permission to use the notice on counterfeit $100 bills.

I am truly grateful to the following at the Shippensburg Health Care Center: Shelly Porter (Unit Manager), Jamie Barnhart, Tammy Batz, Deborah Bercot, Debra Black, Erin Chavez, Deborah Christman, Lori Donovan, Mary Durf, April Etter, Olga Gadomski, Michelle Kelso, Charity Koser, Anna Kriner, Jillian Nicklas, Joy Seavers, Margaret Socha, Kristin Thompson, Traci Walls, and Michaelene Wiesman.

I also want to thank the following at Heartland Hospice Care, Carlisle, Pa. for their kindness and caring: Tracy Fraker, Gloria Krocher, Mary Medkeff-Rose and Robin Zampelli.

My thanks also goes out to the following people who have helped in one-way or another: Shirley Baird, Patricia Coia, Roberta Crumbacher, Barry Dice, Beth Doyle, Glenn Doyle, Donna Gorman, Joann Grandi, Samantha Hockenberry, John Kalathas. Lucas Kalathas, Carol Kerr (Col. USAR Ret.), Katie Kerr, Richard Kerr Sr., Ricky Kerr, Capt. USAF, Rachel Kerr, Joseph McAndrew, Jessica Mickey, Stephanie Misner, CarrieAnn Shay, Kathleen Shay, Nancy Shay, Patrick Shay, and Alannah Staver.

REFERENCES

Cohen, Adam. *Nothing to Fear: FDR's Inner Circle and the Hundred Day That Created Modern America.* New York: The Penguin Press, 2009.

Folsom, Burton W. Jr. *New Deal or Raw Deal? How FDR'S Economic Legacy has Damaged America.* New York: Threshold Editions, A Division of Simon and Schuster, Inc., 2008.

Powell, Jim. *FDR's Folly: How Roosevelt and His New Deal Prolonged the Depression.* New York: Crown Forum, 2003.

Rothbard, Murray. *America's Great Depression.* Kansas City: Sheed and Ward, Inc. Subsidiary of Universal Press Syndicate, 1972.

Shales, Amity. *The Forgotten Man: A New History of the Great Depression.* New York: HarperCollins Publishers, 2007.

Taylor, Nick. *American-Made: The Enduring Legacy of the WPA–When FDR Put the Nation to Work.* New York: Bantam Dell, A Division of Random House, 2008.

Watkins, T. H. *The Hungry Years: A Narrative History of the Great Depression in America.* New York: A Marian Wood Book, Henry Holt and Company, 1999.

Webb, Robert N. *The Bonus March on Washington, D.C. May–June 1932.* New York: Franklin Watts, Inc. 1969.

Westin, Jeane. *Making Do: How Women Survived the '30s.* Chicago: Follett Publishing Company, 1976.

MUSIC

"Brother Can You Spare a Dime?" lyrics by E.Y. Harburg, music by Jay Gorney. Copyright 1932 by Harms, Inc.

"Hobo Blues" by John Lee Hooker.

"Happy Days are Here Again." Music and lyrics by Jack Yellen and Milton Ager, 1929.

PHOTO CREDITS

1, 2, 3. Courtesy of the National Archives. 4. Letter to the Peerless Furniture Company Employees, Courtesy of the Shippensburg Historical Society. 5. Courtesy of the A. P. 6. Courtesy of the *Los Angeles Times*. 7. Courtesy of the Holton Archive/Getty Images. 8, 9, 10. Courtesy of the National Archives. 11. Courtesy of the Library of Congress, Prints and Photographs Division, John Vachon photographer. 12. Courtesy of the National Archives. 13. Courtesy of the National Archives, Theodore Horydczak photographer. 14. Courtesy of the National Archives. 15. Courtesy of the General MacArthur Foundation. 16. Courtesy of the National Archives, Dorothea Lange photographer. 17. Courtesy of the National Archives, Arthur Rothstein photographer. 18. Courtesy of the National Archives, Dorothea Lange photographer. 19, 20, 21, 22. Courtesy of the National Archives. 23. Author photo. 24. Library of Congress, Dorothea Lange photographer. 25, 26. Courtesy of the National Archives. 27, 28. Library of Congress, Dorothea Lange photographer. 29, 30, 31. Courtesy of the National Archives. 32, 33. Courtesy of Wally Baran. 34, 35. Courtesy of the Library of Congress, Prints and Photographs Division. 36. Courtesy of Diane Rooney. 37. Courtesy of Undergroundminers.com. Chris Murley photographer. 38, 39 Courtesy of the National Archives. 40. Courtesy of A.P. 41. Courtesy of the National Archives, Russell Lee photographer. 42, 43 44. Courtesy of the National Archives. 45. Courtesy of the National Archives, Lewis Hine photographer. 46, 47. Courtesy of the National Archives. 48. Courtesy of Vincent J. Genovese. 49. Courtesy of the National Archives. 50. Courtesy of the National Archives, Dorothea Lange photographer. 51. *The Ashland Daily News*, Feb. 1, 1934. 52. Courtesy of the National Archives, Dorothea Lange photographer. 53. Courtesy of the Oakland Museum of California, Paul S. Taylor photographer. 54. Courtesy of the Library of Congress, Prints and Photographs Division, Kristi Finefield. FSA/OWI Collection. [LC-USF 34-9058-C]. 55. Courtesy of the National Archives. 56. Copyright Watch Tower and Tract Society of Pennsylvania. 57. Courtesy of *The Ashland Daily News*. 58, 59. Courtesy of the National Archives. 60. Courtesy of the Library of Congress, Prints and Photographs Division. 61. Courtesy of the Loch Haven Books, Michael Cannon photographer. 62. Courtesy of urbanhomestead.org. 63. Courtesy of the Library of Congress. Prints and Photographs Division. 64. Courtesy of the National Archives. 65. Courtesy of the National Archives, Dorothea Lange Photographer. 66. Courtesy of the National Archives, Walker Evans photographer. 67. Courtesy of blog.craftzine.com. 68. Courtesy of the National Archives. 69. Courtesy of the Arkansas History Commission. 70, 71. Courtesy of the National Archives. 72. Courtesy of victor-victrola.com. 73. Courtesy of Time/Life pictures, George Skadding photographer. 74, 75. Courtesy of the National Archives. 76. Courtesy of Joe Baldino. 77. Courtesy of the Pennsylvania State Archives, A. N. Towsen photographer. 78. Courtesy of Lucas Kalathas. 79, 80. Courtesy of the National Archives. 81. Courtesy of the U. S. Information Agency photo. 82. Courtesy of Shirley Buhl and scanned to me by Joanne Vaughn. 83. Courtesy of the Pennsylvania State Archives. 84. Courtesy of churchfun .com. 85. Oklahomahomeschool.com. 86. Courtesy of the National Archives, Ben Shahn photographer. 87. Courtesy of the Library of Congress, Prints and Photographs Division.

88. Courtesy of the National Archives Dorothea Lange photographer. 89. Courtesy of Wally Baran.

Front cover photo. Library of Congress, P. and P. Division. FSA/OWI Collection. [LC-T01-009095-C] Dorothea Lange photographer. Front cover design by Nick Kalathas.

NOTES

1. On occasion I have altered spelling, punctuation, and capitalization in some newspaper articles for the sake of standardization and readability. I have not, however, changed the substance of any of the newspaper articles in the book.

2. I have attempted to acknowledge and credit all the photographs in the book. I have reviewed hundreds of photos and it is possible that I may have inadvertently omitted a crediting reference. I hope that I will be forgiven if I have accidentally done so.

PEERLESS FURNITURE COMPANY LETTER

November 5, 1930

Mr. Employee, Peerless Furniture Company
Dear Sir:

"Times are hard," economists disagree as to relative statistics; but none may blink the fact that jobs are scarce, and that a man out of employment is out of luck.

Such conditions should force each of us – who have jobs – to take stock of himself. If you are careless, there are dozens of careful men hammering at the doors for your job. If you are disloyal and disgruntled you should get out voluntarily and let a man have the job who would hail it as a godsend.

There need be no secret of the fact that Peerless is "tightening up." Slipshod, careless, indifferent work will no longer be tolerated. Disobedience of orders or regulations will result in instant dismissal. Peerless had reached this stage of the depression with flying colors: she will reach the end of it in exactly the same manner; but only the square shooting employee can be carried with her, and that's that.

You may take this as a plea or a threat, just as you choose. Employees of the Company have not been affected by the depression. You have been having a "boom" period rather than a "panic" – a unusual condition. For your information we insist that a job is a job, now-a-days, and should be valued as such.

Cost of living is coming down – wages, too. New York City paying 10,000 laborers $15.00 per week on city work. Why are you getting more than that?

We have not thought of a general wage cut at this time, we hope the time never comes when some of you have to be cut, but it will come some time. We have, however, a list of about ten men who will be told within the next week to look for other jobs or take a wage reduction, and we tell you now that we prefer your getting another job. The list may grow. Each man determines for himself.

We doubt our ability to keep up night work much longer. Hope we are wrong, but don't think so. A lesson from nature – squirrels put away nuts and bees store honey. Why? Rainy days do come.

This written after careful thought – and for your benefit rather than ours. It's an easy situation for us to handle, we assure you.

Take it, please, as a friendly personal letter.
      Sincerely,
      Peerless Furniture Company
      Carl A. Naugle [President]